Steve Redhead's first book is the product o obsessive love affair with pop and football ture – in roughly equal proportions – for as l as he can remember. He was born in the fift grew up in the sixties, got disillusioned in the seventies, only to stay alive in the eighties: just like modern English football and also – to a lesser extent – pop culture as a whole.

Sing when you're winning
You only sing when you're winning
Sing when you're winning

(terrace chant, anonymous)

Steve Redhead

SING WHEN YOU'RE WINNING

The last football book

Pluto Press

Photo credits

S & G Press Agency Ltd, pp. 2, 11, 15, 24, 29, 31, 32, 33, 37, 43, 52, 59, 60, 67, 72–3, 79, 80–81, 85, 94–5, 103, 109, 130–31, 136, 141.

Sporting Pictures (UK) Ltd, pp. 5, 6, 16, 19, 26, 45, 92, 93, 98–9, 113, 114, 116–17, 124, 128.

Syndication International, pp. 8, 18, 48–9, 70–71, 88, 90–91, 100–101, 106, 142–3.

Kevin Cummins, pp. 66, 69, 82–3.

The Press Association Ltd, pp. 44, 46.

National Film Archive, London, p. 78.

Universal Pictorial Press & Agency Ltd, p. 86.

Dave Thomas Photography, pp. 138–9.

Eamonn McCabe, pp. 54–5.

Football Kick!, p. 51.

Biff Products, p. 38.

Cartoons by R. Lowry.

Book design by Tony Benn.

First published in 1987 by Pluto Press Limited,
6a Noel Street, London W1V 3RB

Copyright © Steve Redhead 1986

7   6   5   4   3   2   1

90   89   88   87   86

Typeset by Rapidset & Design Ltd., London WC1
Printed in Great Britain by Alden Press, Osney Mead, Oxford

British Library Cataloguing in Publication Data
Redhead, Steve
    Sing when you're winning: the last football book.
    1.   Soccer——Great Britain
    I.   Title
    796.334′0941   GV944.G7

ISBN 0 7453 0144 4

Contents

To Ruth and Laura

Acknowledgements

This book would have been impossible without the joint research I did with Eugene McLaughlin. Many people helped in various ways even when they didn't know they were doing so. I especially thank Andrew Ward, Ruth Redhead, Ken Foster, Simon Frith, Robert Adams, Geoff Pearson, Paul Corrigan, Derek Wynne, Simon Turner and Alex Carroll for discussing some of the ideas which eventually found their way into these pages. I am indebted to all those in the football industry who took time out to speak to me. In addition Richard Kuper deserves special thanks for having faith in the original (very different!) project which I pestered him about and for making the writing of the book less of a bind than an evening watching England trying to win the World Cup.

Also, I'd like to acknowledge the contribution of my father, Geoff Redhead, who surely couldn't have envisaged the long-term outcome of taking me to see Blackpool against Newcastle United in 1959! I learnt very quickly about the pleasure (Stanley Matthews) and the pain (Jimmy Scoular) of professional football though the distinction, as the pages of this book testify, was never going to be quite so clear cut again.

Here we go, here we go, here we go

HERE WE GO!! HERE WE GO!!... HERE WE GOOOOOOOOOO?!?!

Football has long been more than a game: when Bill Shankly, Liverpool's legendary manager, claimed that soccer was far more important than life or death, it was an understatement, not an exaggeration. But English professional football in the 1980s is said to be in almost irreversible decline. Shankly's death itself is immortalized in taunting chants and banners from Liverpool's rivals – 'Shankly, Shankly '81', and:

Who's that lying on the roadway?
Who's that lying on the floor?
It's Bill Shankly on his back
And he's had an 'art attack
And he won't be going to Wembley anymore.

The savagery of such retorts is rooted in the underlying social and class changes, economic decline, regional aspiration, deindustrialization, urban decay, and ethnic tension of Britain in the 1980s. Football mirrors, and is mirrored by, society. There are plenty of lasting images and memories from the 1984-5 year-long miners' strike but the football chant 'Here We Go' ringing out on picket lines and football terraces still catches the mood: determined, defiant defence and 'attack, attack, attack', both more in hope than expectation.

It is now over one hundred years since playing soccer for money was legalized in this country and we are certainly light years away from the days in the late 1940s when crowds of well over 60,000 turned out to watch run-of-the-mill Foot-

The good old days

ball League games. But even today the 'beautiful game' provokes extraordinary passions and commitment. In the midst of the worst recession for fifty years, soccer styles, on the field and on the terraces, are once again a major focus of attention. But what makes professional football still so popular? What makes it so special in our culture? What remnants are there from the 'early days' and 'between the wars'? What is soccer's future?

This book prises open the relationship between the seemingly impervious 'football world' and the nightmarish post-1984 circus which goes on unceasingly outside the soccer stadia and the training ground. There are plenty of 'football books', telling us what Kenny Dalglish had for breakfast when he was a toddler or else – at the other extreme – why young working-class males kick the shit out of each other on a Saturday, but few, if any, recognize that there is a connection between the violence and the image of the game. My particular contribution to the pile

of *The Sun Soccer Annual* in summer 'sale' baskets is subtitled 'The Last Football Book' quite deliberately, not because I don't want to read (or write) any more but because the genre, like the game itself, is a gross parody of the original meanings of football as a spectacle for those who watch and play it.

A friend gave me a second-hand bookshop list of 'books about football' while I was writing this book. It contained a reference to Leonard Gribble, *They Kidnapped Stanley Matthews: A Case For Superintendent Anthony Slade* (Jenkins, 1950). I never did get hold of a copy but it struck me that, as Jimmy Greaves once lamented about *playing* the professional game in the 1960s, a certain element of fun has gone out of football writing. I have followed the line of Leonard Gribble (if he ever existed!) and taken much of what is presented as 'fact' about the soccer industry with a lorry-load of salt. The trouble is that if I had ever been able to look inside Gribble's 'fine copy in dust wrappers (torn at lower edge)' I'd probably have found, like Jimmy Greaves if he was really honest, that soccer style in the 1950s was more toiling than triumphant: plenty of 'stopper' centre-halves as well as the odd teasing winger. You can't judge a book by looking at the cover and football's after-the-event notices are notoriously starry-eyed. Indeed, my main argument is that 'football culture' today is massively influenced by the past century of professional soccer and our 'memories' about that history, which (even if we were there) are always mediated, never direct.

Nostalgia in football, a yearning for a Golden Age when fans were peaceful and players were skilful yet obedient servants, is pervasive whether it be in morning newspapers, government reports or John Motson's commentaries. By using 'flashbacks' woven into the narrative account of the modern era since England's victory in the 1966 World Cup I have tried to show

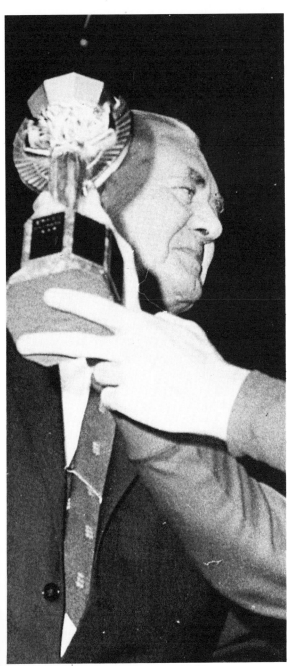
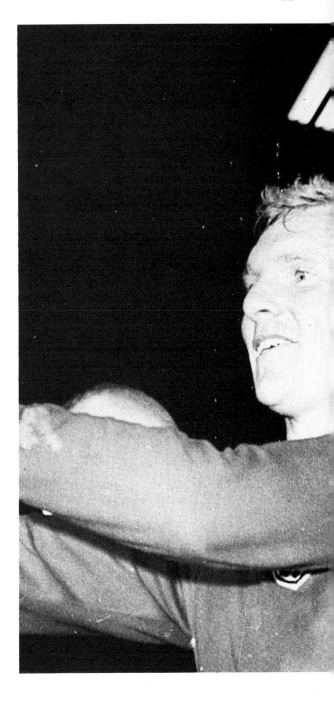

Bobby Moore up for t'cup in 1966

how football passions form a complex web of fact and fiction and sort out what has *really* changed in the hundred years of the industry. The book looks behind the glib notion of 'football madness' to define more precisely than ghosted auto-biographies and academic treatises what it is about football that is a source of pleasure for its remaining millions of participants, spectators and players alike. Drawing on a wide range of material, from interviews with players to novels about football, it tries to capture the flavour of football culture since the ending of the max-imum wage in the 1960s, incorporating *both* the savoury and intolerable aspects of the game, for the two are inseparable. Witty terrace chants are created and sung – more often than not – by the very lads who fight running street battles before and after the match: 'Sing Your Hearts Out For The Lads' and other spectator anthems of the 1980s rapidly degenerate into racial, sexual or political abuse. Equally, the skilful players are frequently those who are identified as 'troublemakers' within the industry. There are no pure elements of football pleasure: joy and strife are two dimensions of the same coin. Further, concentration on 'hooliganism' on the one hand and what top professional players get paid on the other has obscured the thousands of under-rewarded club 'servants' who no one ever reads about and the hundreds of thousands of fans to whom professional soccer is simply their lifeblood.

What is missing from most accounts of foot-ball – give or take the intuition of Hugh McIlvanney or the acute insight of Arthur Hop-craft – is a recognition that the game really is the thing. Soccer *is* all about taking each game as it comes: all the pre-match build up and post-match analysis hinge on the ninety minutes of play. This book consequently ranges over part-icular matches, events and characters (Jimmy Hill plays himself) as well as general issues of

the game in England in the 1980s, such as foot-ball on TV, players' union organization, and vio-lence on the field and off. It suggests connections between soccer and the decline of the nation and points to the international implications of foot-ball chauvinism. Finally, it signals the im-mediate prospects for professional football in its country of origin as we approach the 1990s. ∎

LOWRY

1

Sign on, sign on

" Juventus and Bayern Munich, even Scottish first division bobble hats! Obviously Liverpool are in town.."

How does professional football fit into the contradictions of 1980s England? Conspicuous affluence, yet more than four million on the dole and the nation's most popular spectator sport said to be in its death throes. Football, and footballers in particular, have never exactly been the epitome of style and in a style-obsessed decade that's bad news. George Best in the mid-1960s was the exception rather than the rule as it turned out. The now defunct music magazine *Jamming!* described Best as:

> One of those incomparable individuals – a timely opportune genius. A sixties child. If anything, George Best was *style* pure and simple. Furthermore, like ... great stylists, he found his place in time and created his own legend.

But since Best's heyday players have not very often had the right haircut. Moreover, the media's fascination with the game's origins in long shorts, big boots and flat caps has turned historical memory into a millstone around soccer's neck.

But there are new club cultures hiding beneath the wooden stands, crumbling terraces and steaming bovril. *New Musical Express* described Chelsea's Pat Nevin, a small stylish winger, as the first post-punk footballer and the birth of the Casuals on soccer terraces has given a new dimension to sports and menswear. On top of this, despite notices of its impending demise, professional football is, along with pop music, a key leisure industry serving the youth market. The players themselves are largely between 17 and 35 years old; even younger age groups are the basis of many teams' travelling support, not to mention the vast pool of young television addicts ripe for the merchandizing of football and other products.

Much of the soccer industry seems mercilessly

manipulative. Flair, skill and fun are squeezed out of the game in the relentless search for precious points to stave off relegation. The cliches – 'well, Jimmy', 'take each game as it comes', 'at the end of the day', and all the rest – are churned out for the press, television and radio almost as fast as local businessmen join the board of directors for cheap publicity and a few free tickets. But in the 1980s individual and team styles show some signs of fighting back. Occasionally amongst the flying boots and terrace bloodletting there are glimpses of football 'magic' – the spontaneous excitement generated by a great goal, a defence splitting pass, the 'best save since Gordon Banks from Pele', or merely the biting wit of 20,000 terrace wags which finds it way unedited to the television audience. Those who think this is pure revivalism, though, should think again. Charlie Nicholas is not a new George Best, whatever the media pundits might say; not because their skills don't compare (who can predict what some of the world's clubs could do for Nicholas's flair?) but because this is not a re-run of the 1960s, or for that matter the 1950s, 1940s or 1930s. There is a cutting edge now to winning soccer 'battles', on the field and off.

Style draws

In *The Football Man: People and Passions in Soccer*, one of the few books to capture the flavour of the football culture of its period (albeit one which had disappeared by the time of publication), the journalist and dramatist Arthur Hopcraft wrote:

> Football crowds are never going to sound or look like the hat parade on the club lawns of Cheltenham racecourse. They are

Pat Nevin, Liverpool v. Chelsea, 1985

always going to have more vinegar than Chanel.

The 1970s and 1980s, however, have made Hopcraft's confident late-1960s pronouncement look a little tattered. The football industry is marketing its product for a different type of consumer these days: what that former union leader, Jimmy Hill, has called a 'non-hooligan' audience. Hill's own solution, and much hawked around the boardrooms when he was managing director of Coventry City, was to install an all-seater stadium, the first of its kind in the Football League. The Highfield Road experiment went badly wrong: Man. City and Leeds United fans wrecked it and home supporters protested in no uncertain manner that they had a right to *stand* on the terraces. Also, it's easier said than done to draw Sloane Rangers, yuppies and the rest of the social climbers to an involvement with football in sufficient numbers to displace the proletarian hordes. Soccer is no sport for Young Aspiring Professionals and they are more likely to buy up football clubs than flock to the grounds as paying spectators. Nevertheless, the bedrock of traditional football support – the skilled and white-collar male worker – is drifting away from the turnstiles in large enough numbers to make football's marketing strategists target a richer but also more restricted audience.

If professional soccer in England is still in some way a working-class sport, if it deserves the romanticized description 'the people's game' to any degree at all, it can be partly sensed in its connection with popular music, clothes, fashion. In short *style*. As *The Face*, the magazine most responsible for the rise of style in the recession-devastated 1980s, put it in its fifth anniversary issue:

Style has become the most persistent

cliche and the most powerful currency of our times. In the visual age the look is what really counts . . . But this heightened and even more hedonistic new mod sensibility has taken hold against the backdrop of an economy garotted by Thatcherism.

Robert Elms's view that the 'hero of our times is simply a thief in the right training shoes' denotes a whole football following which is the root of many clubs' home and away support. The emergence of the Casuals, of Terrace Chic, shows how football grounds can become a catwalk for Armani, Lacoste, Fiorucci, Lois, Nike, Farah and Pringle at a time when the game itself is condemned as bankrupt and virtually dead. The dole queue has always beckoned football fans, especially in the period between the wars, but rarely have they celebrated it with such flash and arrogant defiance. Young fans in the 1980s have made travelling to, watching, and travelling back from matches, places to be seen and not just heard (or herded). Kevin Sampson described in *The Face* how, by 1981:

just about every team in the country was able to boast a collection of match-dudes, each trying to outdo the next city in terms of terrace cool . . . I maintain that there are few finer moments in life than when you step into an alien city en masse, all dressed up ruthless, and watch those people *stare*.

Whatever football traditions say about its downmarket origins, soccer now says loud and clear that the way we wear is more important than the way we were.

But where did this obsession with football fashion spring from? What forced this desire to look good on match days as well as Match of the Day?

This dedicated following of style league tables has complex roots, reflecting and inflaming regional and social rivalries in Thatcher's Britain; tensions which surfaced during the miners' strike, leaving Yorkshire teams, like Sheffield Wednesday and Leeds United, firmly identified with Arthur Scargill's line on the dispute. Chants from fans at matches between these teams and clubs from 'moderate' areas like Nottinghamshire and Lancashire were increasingly vitriolic even after the official end of the dispute. Football's latest version of Liverpool's 1960s anthem 'You'll Never Walk Alone':

> Sign on, sign on
> With hope in your hearts
> And you'll never get a job

is the sequel to Alan Bleasdale's *Boys From The Blackstuff*. When sung by Man. United fans to Liverpool supporters it turns up a ratchet the already bitter rivalry between Manchester and Merseyside which produced banners proclaiming 'Munich '58' and 'Shankly '81' towards the end of the 1984-5 season. The same taunts come from London fans, flashing fivers and tenners in front of the tube when Merseyside teams are back in town: just like the Met police used to do on picket lines during the 1984-5 coal strike.

It is not just local derbies, much beloved of television commentators until the trouble starts, that underlie and explain the rush to wear it well or at least better than anybody else. Traditional North-South divides, sharpened by Thatcherism, are stretched to include

nationalist and religious dimensions
   It was no surprise to anyone, apart perhaps
from soccer diarists of the *Guardian*, that it was
a team from north of the border that set the
trends in the 1984-5 season. Unless they were
ball-watching, even those who sit cosseted in the
press box could observe the proliferation of
Celtic ski-hats in the North West following the
Glasgow club's visits to Old Trafford for a match
for Lou Macari (ex-Celtic and Man. United favourite) and the much publicized replayed match
against Rapid Vienna in the European Cup
Winners' Cup.
   The link between Celtic, the Casuals and the
colours was spelt out for *Guardian* readers by a
helpful Merseysider:

> A few years ago the wearing of scarves be-
> came uncool among the 'scallies' and
> others who formed the backbone of away
> support. Then, about four years ago it be-
> came acceptable to wear colours for derby
> games, with bobble hats the most popular
> item. They really took off towards the end
> of last season [1983-4]. With the scallies'
> propensity for wanting to be different, the
> progression to Celtic and Rangers was nat-
> ural. But as with all trends it quickly
> caught on. Now the trick is to come up with
> the most unusual bobble hat. At Liverpool
> games we now see Juventus, German
> teams, some smarties even wearing Aber-
> deen or Hearts hats.

It might be comforting for those who still believe
in the myth of lovable scousers singing witty
songs on the Kop to believe that this is simply
style warfare, but that explanation is as dated

Italian style

Bobble hats

as The Crowd's remake of 'You'll Never Walk Alone'. Although such fads are to some extent market-based – 'it's because they sell them and they are different' – the Catholic connections of Everton, Man. United and Celtic are still strong. Though even they don't reach the heights (or depths) of Rangers' sectarianism which has so obviously attracted Chelsea boys. The flying of Irish tricolours amongst other flags is not entirely innocent or unconnected, and the geographical regrouping (until England versus Scotland matches) of North of England *and* Scotland against the rest is part of a stylistic contempt for self-labelled trendy, fashionable teams and fans of the South. The scallies' move away from Casual to scruffy look in the last couple of seasons is both a reflection of economic circumstances in the region (Adidas, Nike, Lacoste *cost* more) and a desire to keep one step ahead of a style latched onto elsewhere, particularly in the Midlands or South of England. All-black crews at some clubs in the 1980s signal both an organized response to football's racism and a consolidation of black youth's style leadership. Where trends start or who is ahead in the division this month is of course a matter of opinion. Kevin Sampson argued that:

> It was around February of 1978 that this fledgling fashion shook off its punk influences and became more of a cult, a football orientated lifestyle . . . Though drinking, stealing, claiming and clubbing were all important, obsession with clothes gripped young Merseyside something murderous . . . The beginning of the 1979 football season saw the Liverpool look popularized to a national level. Manchester with its 'Perries' and London's 'Chaps' quickly imitated and emulated their scouse rivals by the sheer range of selection and the class of their clothing.

Whether it's flares (trousers not smoke bombs), sun hats, ski-hats, sports or menswear, or whatever; whether it's bought, looted or bought with the proceeds of looting; wherever the location responsible for what the rest of the country does tomorrow, the rise of the Casuals is a savage caricature of the 'affluent' 1980s. How ironic that it was football stadia that saw the development of the flashiest rag trade story since Carnaby Street whilst football's bosses reacted to the game's crisis like a card school on the Titanic. In a nation where the prime minister hardly ventures out of the South East, soccer's style wars are more important than its star wars in the transfer market and the back pages. They take on a new signficance beyond this week's model and football fad leagues. The recession has hit professional football as hard as its major heartlands of the North West, North East, Midlands and parts of the South – not to mention Wales, Scotland and Northern Ireland. It has reduced massively the number of spectators prepared to go out to watch professional soccer matches and decimated the industry's workforce. Style in this context is more than what Simon Frith has called 'bullying clothed in respectability'; it is a postmodern reaction to the death of the modern game.

Modern football

The modern football era begins around the time of England's 1966 victory in the World Cup shortly after the end of the maximum wage system which limited the earnings of soccer players before 1961 and the celebrated court case in 1963, where George Eastham, then of Arsenal, took his former club Newcastle United to the High Court to get a declaration that the old retain and transfer system was illegal. Though these twin bonds of soccer 'slavery' were substantially broken, it did not quite constitut the watershed in football that was claimed at the time as Johnny Haynes of Fulham became the first player to be paid £100 a week and players started to have more freedom to choose who they played for. The transfer system, the chattel market of contemporary soccer, lived on despite the efforts of the players' union, the Professional Footballers' Association (PFA), to get it fundamentally changed.

But, however incompletely, the chains of 'traditional' professional football were shrugged off in the 1960s to produce the modern game: short shorts, lightweight boots and money to burn. The much longed-for 'freedom of contract', players remaining free agents at the end of their contracts with clubs, was won by 1978. But numerous battles to get a European-style 'multiplier' compensation system accepted, based on age, previous experience, status of previous club and salary, have failed miserably. PFA warnings of near collapse of the industry without such a reform have fallen on deaf ears. The big transfer market crash, with the consequent loss of confidence at the banks (players are 'assets' after all) came at the beginning of the 1980s. By 1981 it was being confidently predicted that the days of £1 million-plus transfer deals were numbered but such seven figure sums had only started changing grubby hands in the late 1970s and were on hire purchase or staggered terms anyway, effectively meaning that few if any were actually paid in full. The collapse of transfer values, occurring as it did almost overnight in the 1980-1 season, led directly to clubs, suddenly denied the revenue from the summer and winter sales, cutting costs drastically. Redundancies, severe wage cuts and increasing reliance on part-time and Youth Training Scheme (YTS) players was the result. The crash of Bristol City in 1982 was a warning sign and the PFA's fight for compensation for breach of players' contracts became a *cause célèbre*: the

case of the 'Bristol City Eight', as Peter Ball dubbed the sacked players in *Marxism Today*. Julie Welch, rare token woman in a man's world, said in the *Observer* at the time of the crisis that the club was put:

> on the verge of extinction and eight loyal players in a horrible dilemma ... Geoff Merrick, Chris Garland, Jimmy Mann, David Rodgers, Peter Aitken, Gerry Sweeney, Julian Marshall and Trevor Tainton had contracts worth £290,000; Bristol City, once in the First Division but now in the Third had debts of £1.5 million and assets of £78,000 plus their ground.

Since the winter of 1982 when Bristol City (as was) went down, there have been a string of clubs charging towards the precipice – Hereford United, Derby County, Bradford City, Wigan Athletic, Tranmere Rovers, Wolverhampton Wanderers to name but six. However, only a few 'Ashton Gate Eights' eventually got good, PFA-secured redundancy terms.

This is the context of a renewal of style in professional football in the 1980s: another national industry, a symbol of Britain's manufacturing and imperialist past, teetering on the brink, by its very existence defying economic logic of the Norman Tebbit variety. The modern game was getting its come-uppance with a vengeance and there was a sneaking suspicion that traditionalists as well as Tories were saying 'I told you so'. New football styles, like Watford's version of long ball, kick-and-rush, recalling Stan Cullis's Wolverhampton Wanderers side of the 1950s and Sheffield Wednesday's up-and-under tactic looking like something out of the nineteenth century *before* rugby separated from association football, harked back to the 'good old days'; when men were men, gaffers were gaffers and the 'imported' styles of the 'continent' with their emphasis on a prettier, less masculine form of play could be ignored more readily. The underhandedness of the dirty tricks departments of Italian, Spanish and, especially, South American teams and the political infections of the communist bloc were matched by good old British phlegm, or work-rate as we have come to know it on the football field. Pre-modern times in soccer were characterized by a cultural superiority born of the Empire and a physical toughness hewed out of hard but deferential labour. The 1960s and 1970s sometimes brought an effeminacy to English football styles – just think of Rodney Marsh – which looked positively 'un-British'.

If the modern game's development could somehow be put into reverse maybe the good old days would come again. Perhaps if we dug far enough back into the game's history we could come up with a few Victorian values, even some free-market remedies, which would halt the decline of the industry.

Changes in Football League rules, allowing clubs to keep home gate receipts, have given precisely such a twist to the economic framework of soccer in the mid-1980s. As Tony Mason has pointed out in *New Socialist*:

> Up to 1983-4 the League was a kind of cartel in which some income was redistributed from the better off to the poorer clubs. Home clubs paid a percentage of their gate to the visitors. Money from football pools, club competitions and television was shared out equally to clubs.

However, such distributive justice effectively ended for the 1983-4 season with the Football League's decision to make home teams keep the proceeds of their matches – just what Arsenal, Spurs, Man. United, Liverpool and Everton ordered.

The idea of the rich clubs getting richer, along with the megastars (managers and players) of the game sucking in astronomical salaries (though substantially less than they could make in, say, West Germany, Italy or Spain) accorded very nicely with the life and times of Britain in the grip of boot-boy economics. Kick 'em when you're down made sense even to the non-football followers in the Thatcher cabinet. Thousands of bankruptcies, hundreds of thousands of redundancies in the 'real' world were neatly matched by near bankruptcies and hundreds of sackings in the 'fantasy' world of football. To quote the braying voices on the right side of Fleet Street:

> British football is in crisis: a slum sport played in slum stadiums and increasingly watched by slum people, who deter decent folk from turning up . . . The game needs cleaning up and revitalizing every bit as much as the rest of Victorian industrial Britain. Reassessment should start from the fairly obvious fact that it must stand or fall on its popularity. If people do not want to watch a match then there is no reason in the world why 22 men [sic] should be paid to play it. Football like any other professional entertainment, is nothing if it does not draw crowds on its own merits. Subsidizing entertainment is a contradiction in terms, for if it needs subsidizing it surely cannot be very entertaining.

This aptly entitled *Sunday Times* editorial 'Putting the Boot In', written in the wake of the

Bradford City fire disaster, is made all the harder to resist when football followers are bombarded (usually on the sports pages of the same papers) with the familiar everyday images: of the ungrateful, greedy and overpaid professional footballer who is bleeding the game to death in between getting out of bed with a collection of 'dolly birds' and opening a boutique.

But this is not the whole story. Players' wages in professional soccer are notoriously overstated, given the insecurity they suffer. For the vast majority of Football League professionals the financial rewards are relatively meagre. Not bad in a recession but then footballers have always been better off than many of those who watched them, even in the 1930s under the maximum wage.

The tiny minority of stars and superstars get all the publicity, though is it really Trevor Francis's fault that Man. City *offered* him £2,000 a week to play for them or can Kevin Keegan really be regarded as a culprit when Scottish and Newcastle Breweries are prepared to dig deep for a £3,000 a week handout to recruit him? Such top players inevitably attract the greatest number of outside benefits through advertising and other perks, which doesn't leave much for the majority. When all is said and done, who is going to pay Northampton Town's striker to cavort in the showers with Henry Cooper or tell us what to eat for our tea? Also, the influx on a considerable scale of YTS players into professional clubs has added a new dimension to the old cheap labour scheme (or apprenticeship system as the clubs like to call it): the desire of youth on the dole to play professional soccer is so strong that wages as low as £60 a week were pulling in talent to Second Division sides in the 1984-5 season.

Signing on fees, with, occasionally in the case of big names, massive attendant publicity and glamour poses, have long been a means of off-setting the insecurities of professional football employment, along with other less identifiable and taxable ways of getting in the readies. At one time, especially after 1967 when the PFA negotiated a ten per cent transfer levy – half of which went to the Players' Provident Fund and the other half to the players themselves as long as they did not request the transfer – the professional players had a vested interest in escalating transfer fees. Inflation in the transfer market meant enormous benefits for some footballers without the hassle of actually negotiating a figure for signing on, often the hardest and meanest bargaining in football's industrial relations jungle. But by the 1980 such inequalities were curbed somewhat, with the PFA's successful claim for standardized footballers' pension schemes, achieved only after years of struggle with the Football League and the Inland Revenue, which gave players pension right at 35 years of age. Pensions, funded by contributions, or by League levy on transfers, meant the end of the 'famous international hits hard times' syndrome.

Tommy Lawton, of Chelsea, Everton, Notts County and England, perhaps the best known of this genre, falling right over the moon into the gutter after his playing days, described, in one of football's most poignant autobiographies (usually pulp fiction) *When The Cheering Stopped: The Rise, The Fall* how:

Football carried me to many interesting places, the Kremlin and the Vatican included . . . Life outside the game saw me in the dole queue and the police court, and I ex-

*Tommy
Lawton,
1948*

perienced the doubtful company of bailiffs and debt collectors.

The five per cent portion of transfer fees going to players themselves was curtailed once the new pension scheme was implemented in the wake of the 1978 'freedom of contract' agreement so that old working-class heroes like Lawton would no longer have to sign on at another venue. That did not of course prevent players negotiating signing-on fees individually, or receiving under-the-counter payments or goods for that matter. But the recession has put something of a brake on the sums involved in such deals. Many players are simply glad to have a job. The football revolution which was promised in the context of 1966 and all that may have created the modern game, but that modernism now looks pretty tawdry and the 'people's art', as Hopcraft called it, is in need of radical renewal.

Postmodern football

To ask whether football is actually up or down (market) in the 1980s is not the only gauge of its popularity. In many ways what matters is that it still exists, and, despite various ravages visited upon it, allows relatively cheap entertainment to be served up to mass audience, whether as in the past simply at the ground itself, or, increasingly, on television. The only other comparable industry today is pop music. The link between the two businesses goes back a long way, into the nineteenth century and the origins of professional football and the place of the music hall in popular entertainment.

Julie Burchill's scathing record review of Everton's 1985 FA Cup Final waxing 'Here We Go' put the standard view well – that there is at best a bland, at worst a laughable relationship between football and pop. Burchill wrote in the *NME*:

'Well Brian. Of course you can't entirely divorce football's recent troubles from the social context of unemployment and subsequent frustration in Thatcher's Britain. But a small number of people *are* striking terror into the hearts of people who really love the game.' 'The government, clubs and the public should make it absolutely clear that they are no longer prepared to tolerate football players making records. But what can be done? Electric fences around the recording studios, water cannons at *Top of the Pops*, interviews with Paula Yates? The players themselves should set an example. Take me for instance. I'm opening a boutique, Brian.'

Burchill went beyond this rewrite of a *Monty Python* script to point precisely to this side of football's face:

Everton's chirpy singalong captures the spirit of British football the way *Minder* crystallizes the banality and brutality of the South London underworld.

This mug shot of football is for public consumption only. It depends on the perpetuation of the image of professional footballers as stupid clones only capable of spouting cliched babble. It's what the working class think the middle class want to hear and reflects football culture about as accurately as Joe Gormley singing the Red Flag encapsulates miners' politics. The whole picture of pop's relationship to football is much stranger than this (partial) fiction.

The real identification of football supporters, especially the younger fans, and the players exists in spite of the size of the wage packet and the usually conservative style of most of the game's participants. Fans, in the modern era, have tended to be ahead of the players stylistically, though players are now catching up, opening a cultural pipeline from terrace to pitch which has had some effect on players' tastes and habits, giving new meaning to the old football motto 'its all about the fans'. Until recently the individualist sports like tennis have been the fashion leaders; even the Casuals, though born at the football ground, originally set their sights on tennis gear not football kit. Such fashion trends have been reintroduced into football, copied from other sports and mixed in with the more familiar expression of popular culture on the terraces – the chant.

While Julie Burchill is right to savage football's pop songsters (who could forgive England's 1970 World Cup anthem 'Back Home' and all the remixes and outtakes that it spawned?), the wit and creativity, as well as the violence, of football terraces is legendary. The use of 'live' terrace chants on Sham '69's *Tell Us The Truth* and Pink Floyd's *Meddle* paid musical tribute to this but Jimmy Pursey was simply stealing them, taping the audience's · football choruses, while, predictably, pre-punk hippies went for 'authenticity', taping the terraces themselves. The crossover has, in any case, often been the other way round. Chants come *from* terrace culture; the songs used, from Gerry and the Pacemakers' hit single 'You'll Never Walk Alone' onwards, are simply a vehicle for the frequently spontaneous terrace arguments between rival supporters or between fans and particular players, liked or disliked. The tracks soon got scratched and then deleted, only to reappear in lower division ex-chart bins.

The new pop styles of footballers can be seen as an extension of terrace culture. The music industry's charge to interview anyone who looks like a post-punk footballer makes most football rucks seem tame. Pat Nevin, whose musical tastes initially attracted media attention as much as his wriggling wing play, was proclaimed to be the *first* post-punk footballer by *NME*:

> The last thing he looks like is an average professional footballer . . . out on the park he is one of a rare breed striving to put some joy back into a game slowly choking on its own dour orthodoxy while away from

the field he could hardly be further removed from the sick-as-a-moon-over-the-parrot stereotype of the monosyllabic soccer star.

> An articulate opinionated twenty year old he . . . believes passionately in the anti-nuclear movement and is a discerning follower of contemporary rock music . . . [who] can wax more coherently and enthusiastically about the current music scene than most of the popsters actually involved in it. His passion is that of the true fan.

Nevin has distanced himself from footballers' culture and embraced a lifestyle closer to that of many terrace fans. Like another *NME* interviewee, Ian Stewart of Queen's Park Rangers – whose greatest claim to fame is still that he was sacked for farting in Millwall's assistant manager's car – Nevin sees the players' relationship to the fans as more important than the inward-looking narrowness of the changing room. Stewart thought that:

> the attitude of the players is gradually changing. For three years from 1977 to 1980, the game was getting totally out of hand with all the million pound transfer deals. A lot of players looked down on the fans, but I think that's all over. Football has come down to earth and that's one of the reasons crowds are going up. There are three million unemployed, so footballers cannot afford to think of themselves as anything special.

Setting up his own satirical, jokey fan club is entirely in keeping with Stewart's attitude to other footballers and to supporters, which comes directly out of his background, getting teenage kicks from Belfast punk. Charlie Nicholas, the third of *NME*'s new breed stylists, though perhaps inevitably a more upwardly mobile star has also had, when at Celtic especially:

a unique rapport with the supporters. Although he was out on the field and they were in the crowd, the fans knew that he was really just one of *them*.

Such identity can quickly dissolve as Nicholas found when first Celtic fans and then some sections of Highbury turned against him. Still these skilful, ball-playing Celts stand out from the bunch not just for their flair but in the way they relate to the paying public and especially the young hardcore of matchday supporters. The modern era was supposed to have done away with such traditional football loyalties, based as they were before the 1960s on class and locality. To some extent there was always an element of romantic nonsense in the belief that the past harbours a special relationship between the deferential (mostly) white, working-class footballer and the peaceful (mostly) white, working-class males who flocked to the pleasure domes of industrial England for their weekly fix of the people's opiate. Postmodern footballers, as well as fans, are helping to destroy the myths of traditional as well as modern football watching.

It is the great influx of black English players into the Football League which has, in Robert Elms's words on Garth Crooks, produced a 'new race' of footballers. Elms wrote in *The Face* profile about:

skilful, exciting entertainers who differ from the sadly majestic mavericks who preceded them because of their almost fanatical professionalism. They're athletes, thoroughbreds determined to make the most of their skills and also to make the most out of them. Another thing that's new is that a lot of them are black.

Certainly it is young black players who are now frequently the agents of style, on and off the ball.

There have been black players in League football for decades (Preston North End in the last century and Celtic in the 1950s had black players in their line-up) but the last ten years has witnessed a major transformation, sufficient to provoke Powellite reactions on the terraces and in the clubs. As Peter Ball noted in *Marxism Today* in 1983:

the rise of black footballers has received very visible confirmation in the last twenty months ... Ten years ago the contrast was even more startling with Clyde Best of West Ham the only black footballer appearing regularly in the first division and the widespread prejudice within the game held that black players lacked the moral and physical toughness, 'the bottle' in football jargon, to survive in the Football League.

Racism on and off the terraces is endemic in football, though it isn't always courtesy merely of the touchline fascists. John Bond's televised comments about his own player, Dave Bennett, when he was manager of Man. City for the 1981 FA Cup Final summarise the subconscious depths of traditional football attitudes:

like a lot of coloured players in this country ... you pull your hair out with them ... they drive you mad ... he's got so much ability and so much potential.

Bond's fellow medallion man, Ron Atkinson, had the gall to relay to television's millions that Brendan Batson, his player at Cambridge United and West Bromwich Albion, had, typically a chip on his shoulder about his colour. With

*Garth
Crooks
shadowed
by Willie
Young,
1980*

friendly managers like these who needs enemies on the terraces?

Yet the distinctiveness of black players is not just individual flair but their contribution to team styles in the 1980s. The recent predictions of an all-black England football team by 1990 are starting to look a little premature with the constant undermining, by media experts, of the 'staying power' of flair players (i.e. black players, *plus* Hoddle and Francis) at national level. Michel Platini eat your heart out! However, in the modern era's last fling, black players' contribution to changes in English football style has been significant. Following England's World Cup victory in 1966, Alf Ramsey's shameful shunning of Jimmy Greaves (shoving in Geoff Hurst as an afterthought) became a tactical blueprint: hard-running, wingless wonders crawled out of their dug-outs and team work got rave notices. The national side's dourness was seen as reflecting Ramsey's taciturn, brusque style with the press, albeit absurdly searching for upper-class speech patterns and ending up, like his later teams, something of a poor man's joke. Leeds United, under the management of Don Revie, and to some extent Liverpool under Bill Shankly, created action replays of England at club level contrasting sharply with the stylish, attacking team of Matt Busby at Man. United. (Where are they now? No 1: John Aston, winged terror of Benfica at Wembley in 1968 – selling dog biscuits in a Derbyshire market.) Leeds and Liverpool took aspects of Ramsey's 'professionalism' into new, uncharted waters at club level and into European competition equating success with absence of flair. Arsenal's double side of the 1970s, and later Nottingham Forest, carried on the tradition. Not that these sides didn't contain players who could 'entertain' or turn a game in a second; more that they couldn't *only* do that, or they wouldn't get picked.

Foul magazine, football's equivalent to *Private Eye* in the early 1970s, served as a protest against the years of boring, defensive, dull, dirty team styles which mushroomed after 1966. It remains one of the few radical attempts to intervene, however jokily, in professional soccer in Britain. It reflected a moment in the history of the game but left simply a temporary monument to the reaction against the tactical stifling of skill and flair. Style and the game had already moved on by the time a collection of *Foul* oldies came out in 1976. In many ways it represented a hippy, 1960s backlash to the end of that decade: the demise of George Best was the equivalent of the Rolling Stones at Altamont or the Manson family's killing of Sharon Tate. The nostalgia compares with Terry Venables's futuristic novel about football, written with *Hazel* collaborator Gordon Williams. *They Used To Play On Grass* looked backwards to a mythical paradise of skill and style before Venables burst onto the scene with Peter Bonetti, Jimmy Greaves and the rest of Ted Drake's Ducklings in the late 1950s. Venables and Williams's prophetic predictions – ironically El Tel was later to manage Queen's Park Rangers, the first English team to introduce us to the pleasures of the plastic pitch – are mixed in with a longing for more memorable soccer styles of the past. A character in the book fondly recalls the 'glory days' when they used to play on grass:

and there on the pitch he began to see players from his past, still doing the things that gave the game its magic . . . he saw the salmon leap of Dennis Law, the Viking Scot . . . he saw Jimmy Greaves, the little man, gliding past slicing boots and scything legs on a deadly run to goal, protected by invisible rays . . . he saw the silky poetry of Alec Young, the man they called the Golden Vision . . . he saw the flowing hair of George Best, the little boy genius who had it all . . . he saw Bobby Charlton, pride of England.

Today, less fictional characters than this fan are indulging in the same vain search for a lost fantasy world.

Football in the 1970s and the 1980s to some extent mirrors changes in pop styles. 'Authentic' rock music, which emanated from the counter culture of the 1960s, was seen, in the 1970s, to be eclipsed by 'commercial' pop. In the mid-1980s a 'new authenticity' is in vogue, a resurrection of guitar bands and singer/songwriters as if synthesizers and drum machines had never killed them off in the first place. A champion of 'authenticity' throughout this period, from the 1960s to today, on both football and pop fronts, disc jockey John Peel has argued for *real* football. He contended in *City Limits* in 1983 that:

football does not need brightening up, at least not in the way Jimmy [Hill] and his chums advocate . . . No, we must unite, brothers and sisters, against those who would wreck football. And who are those wreckers? I hear you cry. I name the football authorities and a disturbing number of those who report and comment on the game . . . When experts discuss the critical lack of interest in football . . . they overlook

Dennis Law

Jimmy Greaves in Chelsea days, 1957

– or dare not suggest – that those who run the clubs . . . are woefully out of touch. In their anxiety to milk revenue from the game before it collapses completely, they make decisions which alienate the most dedicated of fans.

Though Peel argues that radical rethinking is necessary for football to survive, he rejects modernizing schemes which will irrevocably give football crowds more 'class'. There is an assumption that we know what real football essentially is, just as we know what authentic, real pop music sounds like. But where is the divide between plastic and authentic? Were directors and administrators more in touch in the 1960s? Were Jimmy Hill's modernizing plans not hatched at Coventry City some twenty years ago along with Harold Wilson's white heat of technology in industry?

The problem for football is that it never had a punk phase. There has never been such a radical break in soccer styles as in pop. You can't talk of pre-punk football and post-punk football in quite the same way as you can about pre-1976 and post-Sex Pistols divisions in musical styles. David Lacey described Everton's League and European Cup Winners' Cup side of 1984-5 in the *Guardian* as the:

> team of the 80s – not in their tactics which owe something to the Liverpool style of fifteen years ago – but in their attitude. They are a blue overall side who have given work rate a better name.

Lacey contrasted this team with the last time the club won the League championship in 1970, at the end of a period 'when the pursuit of money outweighed everything else'. In the *Jamming!* interview with George Best the player was said to have taken:

Jimmy Hill, 1960

football in the early sixties – when the game was beginning to give in to a tactical back-room lukewarmness, as imagination submitted to big business – and almost single-handedly provided its life support of character, colour and unconventionality.

1960s heroes like Best and Greaves – along with the likes of Law, Venables and others who lingered on to the middle of the 1970s – are now making curtain calls in the media, beckoned on as representing the essential, authentic dimension of professional football *before* the modern era really took hold. They are seen as throwbacks to the traditional era who were mangled by commercial exploitation and defensive tactics; in the tragic cases of Best and Greaves driven into alcoholism and a very early bath when their careers should have been peaking. This view of authenticity doesn't however allow for changes in fitness, style of dress, pattern of play and so on. Greaves to his credit though still maintaining that 'years ago there were more thrills and spills' acknowledged in a *City Limits* interview that:

> It's totally different. Players are fitter, more versatile – when I played, you could tell a full back by size, height and weight – and better pitches and playing gear all go to help. But then you've created stalemate.

It is the dead weight of traditional memory which is killing soccer every bit as much as hooliganism and get rich quick merchants. Team and individual styles have clearly fluctuated since the late 1950s but there is no easy return to authentic football when post-punk footballers take the field. It is literally a different ball game from the heady days of flower power which spawned the 1970s critics of the spectacle of professional soccer. ■

2

Munich, Munich '58

" You're not wearing Brylcreem and you haven't even had a shave ! What are you trying to do, young man, bring the name of the game into disrepute?! "

Ten years is a long time in football: about as long as a week in politics. But a diary of the 1974-5 season looks remarkably similar to one written in the mid-1980s. There were pitch invasions, crowd trouble abroad, player indiscipline, government concern with hooliganism and the decline of the 'national' game – its image, number of paying spectators, performance of the England team and so on. A hundred years ago, too, there were magazine articles criticizing professional footballers for their supposed greed, laziness and bad example. Even so a powerful, seductive image of the 'past' as a Golden Age of English football constantly recurs. Nostalgia for a moment in the game's history is ever-present, even if the particular period in question is always debated. Was English football better in the 1920s, 1930s or 1950s or even in Edwardian times? When Charlton Athletic moved from their 'historic' Valley stadium in the 1985-6 season to cross over to Crystal Palace's Selhurst Park, for what promised to be the first of many long-term ground sharing schemes, the tears flowed and anger raged. Old memories were stirred; as John Jackson of the *Mirror* told us:

> I still remember cramming myself onto that towering terrace for a match against Arsenal in 1956 when the gates were shut after 70,000 people had clicked through the turnstiles . . .
> . . . Seventy year old Sailor Brown joined many old players introduced to the crowd on Saturday. He said: 'I looked up at the huge terrace and I heard the roar of 70,000 throats'.

But with those glory, glory days fading fast from Jackson's memory rewind he noted that 'today's football climate with its hooliganism and anti-social behaviour would not allow such a crowd'.

The death of the Valley, moreover, signified the state of the nation's football:

> British soccer is going bust. The decision by Charlton Athletic and Crystal Palace to share one ground seven miles away at Selhurst Park may well be prophetic . . . As Ted Croker, once a Charlton player, now secretary of the Football Association, said, 'This could be the beginning of a new era. If this sort of move can defray the costs for a club, then it must be good. Loyalty and traditions die hard. I am just sad that the guinea pig is my old club.'. . . Television personality Jimmy Hill, a Charlton director, faced mobs of angry supporters on Saturday. They wore black ties, laid wreaths on the centre spot and held a sit-in on the pitch at half-time. And when the final whistle had blown, they took away lumps of turf for keepsakes. Hill said, 'This sort of decision is never easy, but lack of money makes it inevitable' . . . Emotion at times washed away the talk of the hard realities of soccer life.

This is now a pervasive theme in professional football. It is a familiar romantic picture of soccer history, bordering on the sentimental if not the downright fantastic. It rapidly becomes contrasted with a 'realism' which boards of directors of Football League clubs and the governing bodies, namely the Football League and Football Association, are said to be applying in order that professional football in its 'mother

'Charlton v. Stoke. Last day at the Valley. 63-year-old William Hopper from Peckham who has been a supporter for 49 years surrounded by young Charlton supporters. He cut a piece of turf as a keepsake, as his team played their last match at the Valley.' – Sport and General

country' might hobble on crutches towards 2000. Soccer styles, on and off the pitch, are themselves prisoners of the past. Nostalgia OK?! But was football more entertaining when players were poorer and more deferential? Were they more patriotic? What did centre partings, Brylcreem, dubbin and leather 'casies' have to do with style?

Putting on the agony

When skiffle hero Lonnie Donegan's single 'Gambling Man/Putting On The Style' was in the charts in 1957, football was about to enter a critical phase. Football in the 1950s, even if that description cut into the next decade to include the 'traditional' footballers of Tottenham Hotspur's double-winning side of 1961, was significant for at least two reasons. It is just about within the recall of popular memory of many older present day fans *and* it is the last time soccer players are generally regarded as having a legitimate grievance over wages and conditions. Spurs' side of the early 1960s, built in the 1950s on the maximum wage system, was the last of the great British club sides to be viewed with pure nostalgia – later teams' success was always tinged with media suspicion of players who were 'greedy' or who made 'outrageous' wage demands. (These had by now become known as 'salary claims'.)

David Lacey, reviewing manager Bill Nicholson's autobiography *Glory, Glory – My Life With Spurs* for the *Guardian*, recalled the context of the League and Cup double side's triumph:

> Then, as now, football was in decline. The Munich air crash of 1958 had destroyed Manchester United, who represented the domestic game's brightest future, and Wolverhampton Wanderers, while still successful, were no longer the force they

had been for most of the 1950s . . . The quality of Tottenham's play, the individual skills of Blanchflower, White, Mackay, Smith and Jones, which were harnessed to the team effort without ever being stifled by it, gave those fortunate enough to witness their matches the feeling that English League football was being reborn. Now we know that Spurs' Double was really marking the end of an era.

Lacey's review proceeded to stress forcefully the argument that the 1961 abolition of the maximum wage and the 1963 Eastham court case were to make it impossible for teams ever again to be constructed on this model. Generous – in Lacey's view – salaries, freedom of contract and the 'fear of failure and financial loss which soon began to be reflected in negative attitudes on the field after the Double season', have made it extremely difficult for teams to be entertaining and successful'.

This is not all idle sentiment; there is a kernel of rationality here amongst Lacey's look back in anger at today's football flaws. Clearly the 'trad' era did in some senses experience its finale with the onset of the mid-1960s, which ushered in a 'mod' phase, generally characterized by negativity. But at the same time, Lacey, like numerous other commentators and spectators who watched the 1950s style as it developed out of the post-war 'austerity', joins Nicholson himself in a romantic dreamworld, swallowing the belief that standardized wages in themselves gave teams their essential morale, spirit and indeed 'democracy', leaving them distinguishable from the spectating public only by their 'skill'.

Such mythology is pernicious and has helped football clubs enormously in their staunch fight against both the abolition of the maximum wage and the winning of freedom of contract in limited form. It has given sustenance to former Football League secretary Alan Hardaker's view that the ending of the maximum wage had something of the status of a crime against humanity and should never be accepted as a *fait accompli*. Similar myth-making has underscored the performance of England's national team in the modern era which, of course, virtually opened with its last triumph – the winning of the World Cup in 1966. In 1981, in what was widely seen in the media as an ignominious defeat by Norway – amidst much re-running of a Norwegian television commentator's shrieks of euphoria and roll-call of English 'heroes' of yesteryear from Winston Churchill to Margaret Thatcher – Jeff Powell of the *Daily Mail* piled the increased payments to players for international appearances in England on top of 'high' club wages as the reason for failure. In one sense this was just another World Cup-qualifying 'slip-up' against a 'small' nation only fit for fiords and rally-driving, familiar fodder for the daily press still dozily dreaming of Empire days, but Powell really went to town. Instead of accepting that England's 1966 performance was overvalued and that previously 'soft-touch' nations were rapidly catching up those fortunate enough to be considered worthy of World Cup seeding, our journalistic hero launched a scathing attack on 'greedy, unpatriotic, overpaid and over there' international stars who in his opinion should play for England for nothing. Lessons in the evils of Mammon when playing for the old country were probably less relevant than asking which players had been on the bevvy the night before because they believed everything they read in the papers about their 'part-time' opponents and reckoned they could risk it.

The nostalgia for pre-modern days was once more irresistible and who should the *Mail* wheel out to wallow in it but one of the major names on the Norwegian commentator's list – that born-again midfielder who gave Ramsey's wingless wonders a touch of class, Bobby Charlton. Charlton recalled an earlier international – and domestic – era after the Second World War and before the abolition of the maximum wage in the early 1960s. What characterized this period for Charlton, who came into the profession in the tail end of these years, was the lack of social distance between the players and supporters, connected inextricably, in Charlton's mind, to performance. In an article attributed to *Mail* man John Roberts and Charlton himself, entitled 'England, My England', the argument ran that 'the public have lost their sympathy with footballers . . . [j]ust after the war players seemed to belong to the society in which they played'. As Jeff Powell had already said in the same sports pages that day 'Blame The Money!' But just as the nation's 'shameful' defeats in the 1950s – first by the USA and then later in some style by Hungary (twice), for instance – seemed to have escaped the old international's memory, so the exact connections between fans, players and clubs got somewhat clouded in the mists of time. If anything captured the professional footballer's life and times in the 1950s in England it was that curious combination of deference with 'respectability'. Stanley Matthews, 'Mr Football' of the day, put it best in his early autobiography *Feet First Again* (Corgi special, 2s 6d, 1955):

I am grateful also to the Football Association and appreciated the address and the certificates presented to me when I broke

'Mr Football'

the international appearances record. Football has been kind to me. But most important of it all it has provided me with thousands of true friends. They are on the terraces each week.

Matthews's own pristine reputation was to be somewhat tarnished by football scandal in later years but his view from the mid-1950s reeked of servility: a humble worker who knew his place and was grateful for any extra crumbs that fell off the top table. No one who saw Matthews in the flesh could forget his dribbling skill – though he didn't exactly head the ball very often! – but it was the ideal picture of the traditional footballer which he represented that makes his deference so significant. It's precisely that style of club 'servant' that many of the radical reforms being contemplated by football's current masters are designed to resurrect. Skilful and dutiful: a winning combination!

Many of the crop of sociological studies of football are tarnished by this same romantic brush, though they are just as often coloured by a strongly expressed passion for players' rights. Their nostalgia for the past – and particularly the 1950s – comes from seeing in players like Matthews, figures with impeccable (manual) working-class credentials, before they had become 'seduced' by the 1960s and 1970s. The problem is that things were never that clear cut (Matthews father, for instance, may have been a boxer but he also owned his own barber's shop) and it was not always possible to describe players as if they'd just come off the night shift. Even the most observant of football's critics tend to romanticize the class origins of footballers, as David Triesman did in his introduction to Gerhard Vinnai's *Football Mania*. Recalling – from the 1950s, where else? – the 'Lion of Vienna', otherwise known as Nat Lofthouse, Triesman wrote of:

> a player who . . . had been a Bevin boy in the last war, a coal pit face worker conscripted for work in the mines rather than military service. Lofthouse, like so many other footballers came off the terraces, the son of a coal man, and he went into first-class football on a £1 10s 0d weekly wage.

You can almost hear the accompanying strains of the Hovis advert which Southern fans now use to taunt crews from the North, particularly if they're not looking good that week, recycling the past for present consumption.

Another of football's better chroniclers, David Robins, has published the oral testimony of a Man. City fan who remembers the era of the 1940s and 1950s when Maine Road had:

> a very mixed crowd. There was a lot of old blokes, and women, even some elderly women. You all stood there together. You knew everybody. You never saw 'em between games. But we always stood in roughly the same place and we knew the forty or fifty people around us 'cos they were always there. The worst hazard of standing in that crowd was someone pissing down the back of your leg. But now it's getting a bottle on your head and that's a different thing altogether. It takes the fun out of it.

Ah! the good old, bad old days: when players were big and strong and working class, and being pissed wet through meant exactly what it said!

What's at issue is not that such descriptions provided a completely false picture of particular aspects of professional football in the 1950s. But they are taken as representing *general* trends which postmodern football has seen off with all the contempt for social history it can muster. These myths of idealized traditional football persisted well into the modern era in the 1960s and 1970s.

Only when football clubs started to modernize amenities like bars and toilet facilities for the mass of fans did the image of 20,000 Kop-ites carrying their rolled up match programmes in case they got caught short before half-time become well and truly a thing of the past. None of the modernizing of football means that fans cannot stand together in the same place on the terraces (or sit in the seats) year after year enjoying the gentle sarcasm of the crowd, the pathetic failure of their team to score or the brilliance of the away team's goalkeeper. Unless the modernizer is Jimmy Hill (and there are plenty more where he came from) claiming to rescue the traditional game from 'hooliganism' while, at the same time, vandalizing every terrace in sight to get more 'bums on seats' and more money in the bank.

More important than all this, though, is th view of the late 1950s as the moment in th game when the uncoached, natural football ability of the working man made virtually its last stand, before it surrendered – irrevocably? – to the modern era, with its master coaches (Allison, Revie, Greenwood, Howe and Robson) ready and waiting to confuse it out of them. The notion that only the modern era has witnessed the appliance of science (tactics, drawing boards, team dossiers and all the rest) is a historical fiction but the memory lingers on of the day an era died: the Munich air disaster which called an abrupt end to the 'Busby babes' of Man. United. The team containing Duncan Edwards hangs like a mural over Old Trafford even today. The death of many of Busby's brightest hopes (and the survival of Busby himself and Bobby Charlton) symbolized both the fracturing of traditional football style and the rebirth of its most significant component – the umbilical cord between soccer fans and 'entertaining' football – in a much more hostile decade. Eclipsing the memory of even the great United side of the late 1940s, the 1958 air crash almost alone established Man. United's awesome pulling power which has drawn enormous support for the last thirty years. It simultaneously lit the fuse of rivalries already burning (in the city of Manchester, between Manchester and Merseyside and between the North on the one hand and the Midlands and the South on the other) which have exploded in the 'hooligan' battles of the 1970s and 1980s.

'We only hate Man. United,' has echoed the reaction of thousands of spectators when this Red Army has come to, or crossed, town in modern times. The widespread journalistic shock horror reporting of 'Munich '58' banners on Merseyside in 1984 and 1985 as if it was the ultimate football insult (to rank alongside Liverpool's banners proclaiming that 'Atkinson's got AIDS' at a televized 'live' FA Cup game at Barnsley) is both deeply hypocritical – people in per-

spex press boxes shouldn't throw stones – and a sign of how out of touch sports reporting has become. The fact that United's average gates were almost twice as high as most of their First Div-

Bobby Charlton (Man. United), with hair, v. Maurice Norman (Spurs)

Munich airport, 6 February 1958

ision competitors in the 1985-6 season, and increasing whilst everybody else's have declined, is still linked to the Munich disaster, however tenuously. Fans in every port, coaches from all over the country in the car park at every home match, United are a 'national' team. Their style since the Munich days has been ever more 'business-like' (complete with scandal surrounding the club under the chairmanship of Louis Edwards) off the field and for the most part attacking on it. A 'multi-national' giant corporation (along with perhaps Liverpool, Arsenal, Everton and Spurs in the 1980s) in a sea of small shopkeepers; a commitment to positive football with flair in an era when not losing has always been more important – that is, 'getting a result'. Mass public sympathy for the terrible loss of virtually a whole team in an unnatural tragedy has been translated into an association of their team and individual styles with 'going forward' (it is always United's attacking players that are re-

called: Law, Best, Charlton – not Sadler, Brennan, Dunne) to such an extent that Dave Sexton's 'modernist' style cost him the managerial chair at Old Trafford. It is still remarkable how the ghostly presence of the 'lost' team – particularly Duncan Edwards – haunts even the present day United team; how even the physical qualities (thick thighs, tough tackles and a general air of power) of Bryan Robson, Mark Hughes and especially Norman Whiteside recall for watching journalists the days before the screen test for Airport '58. Even the 1960s side was always fettered by United manager Matt Busby's much proclaimed need to win the European Cup, which was seen to be so near when the 1950s team crashed, and by his desire to avenge deep anger, personal grief and public loss. The final closure of the story, the 1968 European Cup Final victory at Wembley over Benfica (or Stiles over Eusebio), was achieved at the cost of killing another team, less painfully

but just as surely, with its most prominent individualist, George Best, sliding into despair. As Best remembered in his third, and apparently most truthful, autobiography *Where Do I Go From Here?*, after the 1968 win:

> The adrenalin slowed and I could feel myself no longer part of the laughter and the tears. I was there but I didn't belong. All around me were men and women for whom this was the greatest night of their lives; the climax of all the years of planning, tragedy, disappointment and determination. It should have been that for me. Instead, although I was not to know it at the time, it was the beginning of the end.

Busby's mission accomplished, Best slipped down the grassy slope of success as he witnessed the break-up of the team which came on as substitutes after 1958. In a way this was 'traditional' football's encore.

Won't get fouled again

Man. City fans' taunting their 'Manc' rivals in the mid-1980s with 'There's only one United – a biscuit' and 'You only came in a taxi' might have found their way on to the pages of football's only 'alternative' paper *Foul* if Stan Hey and Andrew Nickolds had not gone on to pastures new in television drama/sitcom. Apart from rare instances in fanzines, it has been left to 'what's on' rags in London and the provinces – *City Limits, Time Out* and all the clones – and the occasional ill-fated radical paper like the *Leveller* or *Rolling Stone*-lookalike *Street Life* to open up football culture. *Foul*, in name certainly, protested about the dirty tricks abounding in professional soccer styles at the beginning of the 1970s – previously associated with 'overseas' players – which Billy Bremner and the 1960s boys per-

George Best: no regrets?

Jimmy Guthrie, chair of the Players' Union, before the fall

It was the calculating collaboration of so many of the game's participants in its (alleged) stylistic decline which motivated the mixture of satire and investigative journalism that graced *Foul*'s pages between 1972 and 1976. But the whole ethos of the magazine was still fatally hamstrung by a nostalgia for a bygone era. Though geared to a defence of the 1960s 'stylists', it pined for that mythical Golden Age of the 1950s as if the long march of football talent ended, or went into reverse, when Jimmy Guthrie was allegedly 'stabbed in the back' by the Players Union and was unceremoniously succeeded by smooth-talking, upwardly mobile Jimmy Hill. A late issue of the mag in October 1976 carried an interview with the former Portsmouth player whose self-styled 'militancy' has become something of a yardstick used to beat any of the so-called 'moderates' who live in the shadow of his chairmanship of the Players Union in the 1940s and 1950s. The occasion was the publication of his autobiography *Soccer Rebel* and Alan Stewart's article on Guthrie concluded that:

> the book serves to remind the present smug and apathetic leadership of the PFA that the Union did once have a more radical chairman, and that the ideal of winning the war in order to disband the army is not one to be despised.

Foul frequently lashed the PFA ('Pretty Feeble Altogether') in the 1970s – the then chairman Derek Dougan was a favourite target – for weakness and for using the official positions of the organization for self-aggrandizement – going into television, management or business. Guthrie certainly claimed that his sole aim was to make the Union's function redundant – in his words 'to make footballers free' – and courted the labour and trade-union movement like no

formed eagerly, but it wasn't simply the roughness and cynicism seeping into Britain's premier spectator sport that was at stake. No one was actually being killed and there had already been plenty of ruthless 'cloggers' in football's history.

other Union footballer since Charlie Roberts. But the fact is that he frequently lost the confidence of the Players Union management committee and it was Hill who successfully negotiated the conditions of a new era after Guthrie's acrimonious departure. It is perhaps no accident that it was the captain of Spurs' double side, Danny Blanchflower, who wrote the foreword to Guthrie's book; for as Blanchflower is remembered as the skilled leader of the last great football *club* team of working class heroes, and Stanley Matthews revered as last of the dignified, deferential master craftsmen of the 'art' of professional soccer, Jimmy Guthrie is resurrected as the last great politically conscious 'traditional' footballer. After Guthrie, the story goes, the Union became an 'Association' and was the midwife to a 'middle-class' footballer who wanted none of Guthrie's principles of collective solidarity with 'the people' who paid to watch the game.

Foul's much needed, and much missed, irreverence about the soccer world shrouded a naivety about football politics which assumed that the 1950s battles to abolish the maximum wage and the retain and transfer system, which Guthrie led with such militant rhetoric, were conducted in something like an age of innocence. It was the replaying of these past 'heroic' struggles on the modern football stage which brought forth such venom, especially against the PFA, which was seen as selling out the members at every turn since the early 1960s. It gave players such as Eamon Dunphy (whose diary of part of a season still stands as a far more accurate 'day in the life of a professional footballer' than all the glossy 'biopics' put together) space to sharpen their pens. It gave journalists of stature in later years – Peter Ball (who collaborated with Dunphy) and Chris Lightbown – the opportunity to develop new insights on soccer culture, particularly press reporting.

But it was still based on the notion that if only the classic militant trade unionist had not been extinguished from PFA ranks, footballers really would be free. *Foul* itself harked back to Guthrie's era when skill was seen to triumph even if it was because full backs and centre halves were too slow and clumsy to catch flying wingers and tricky inside forwards. But the death agonies of modern football were still to come when *Foul* was busily building itself as 'Football's Alternative Paper' in the early 1970s.

Foul magazine in many ways served as a warning of what was to come. It said what mainly young middle-class fans said on the terraces every Saturday during the 1970s; it just said it in a *Private Eye* format (unsurprisingly – it was typeset at the same place!) and ridiculed everything and anybody in its wake with a cheerful disregard for propriety. It was a forum too for those who argued for 'real' football watching: ten years before John Peel's Campaign for Real Football a *Foul* correspondent complained:

What the hell is all this we keep hearing about 'Family Football', 'More Seated Accommodation' and 'Restrict Movement on the Terraces'? Is this the fate for football in the future? The Game seems to be turning its back on the real supporters in favour of the Season Ticket family and their admittedly greater money. But will they, Mum, Dad, Auntie Doris and the kids, go to a game in the middle of winter at the other end of the country when there is a rail

strike on? Will they Hell!

Football is not about covered stadiums, padded seats, ice cream and women and kids. It's about hitching, getting pissed, shouting, standing, pushing, pissing on your boots or the guy in front's legs, singing, chanting, surging and swaying, scarves and if you feel like it AGGRO!

The more we try and make the middle class frightened of coming to games, the more they are excluding us, fencing us in and restricting our movement on the terraces. So bad is this getting that they have put up barriers on the Kop to stop that famous glorious surge. What next? A ban on singing? No scarves allowed? No standing room? It's coming unless we do something about it.

Chanel O Vinegar 3! A scoreline which was to be reversed in the replay by the 1980s. An even more anarchistic vision of the possibilities of 'fighting back' rather than 'each other' by another letter writer to *Foul* – who thought that 'we should be uniting in hundreds of thousands as defiant, resentful kids' not 'blindly and fearfully lashing out at anything that wears the wrong colour scarf' – sketched in what the young 'pissed-on' males of British soccer should beware:

Apparently well-meaning chaps like Gordon Jago and Jimmy Hill will *destroy* football if allowed any sort of administrative power. Their Utopia is a spotless concrete bowl lined with thousands of little blue plastic seats, lots of clean toilets, a restaurant, a sports complex, piped muzak, and 22 clean-cut, goal-hungry young zombies playing the game in a spirit of

friendship and sportsmanship on a plasti-grass pitch. They want matches which end in 7-7 draws, watched by packed crowds of middle class parents who have each brought their 2.4 children who cheer enthusiastically every goal, applaud every exhibition of skill from the opposition and who go home afterwards in their family saloons, all agreeing that they have been thoroughly entertained.

Bollocks to their visions! It is on those cold forbidding terraces that you find the central nervous system of football from which the adrenalin rises and the lifeblood flows.

But in the 1970s, modernization of the industry already took these backward glances (to the days when mothers, wives and girlfriends sat at home waiting for their young men to come back from the football front) by the scruff of the neck and exposed their political strategy for the empty clap-trap that they implied about the power of 'the working class' in soccer; as surely as the 1979 Thatcher government smashed the complacent belief in the unstoppable forward march of British labour.

Foul was certainly not alone in its counter-cultural criticisms of football based on a romantic picture of the past. The *Leveller* was bitten by the same bug. Its pilot issue in February 1976 even managed to discover an inheritor of the Jimmy Guthrie tradition, though it had to go to Scotland, where the Scottish PFA had recently affiliated to the General and Municipal Workers' Union (as it was then), to interview Jackie McNamara one of Celtic's rare breed – a member of the Communist Party of Great Britain. When asked how far he had succeeded in convincing his team-mates to support the 'working-class struggle' McNamara replied wearily:

I have tried the odd time, but you just get shut up right away because they're not interested, they're detached from the struggle. I can only talk about Celtic Park. There aren't many who are politically conscious at all. They are in it for the wages and that's all.

Beyond the *Leveller*'s Red Clyde nostalgia was recognition that the 'freedom of contract' dispute, in its bitterest phase, was more than just a sell-out by the union. In a piece entitled 'We was Robbed', John Allen highlighted Steve Perryman (one of another dying species: the Labour-voting Spurs player, identified by Hunter Davies in *The Glory Game*, a year in the life of the club at the beginning of the 1970s) as emphasizing the more serious side of footballer insecurity when he spelt out the soccer player's lot: 'I talk about going to work and people laugh, they think you just kick a ball around on a Saturday afternoon'. Allen noted that even in 1977:

The popular image, heroes of the working class getting rich quick for working 1½ hours a week, and the entrenched attitudes of the game's governing body, the Football League (an autocratic body of employers – club chairpersons who look after the game in their spare time), have resulted in feudal working conditions for professional footballers. Treated as fleshy capital, investments who only think through their feet, they are unable to change jobs without their current employer demanding cash from their would-be employer. No other worker in Britain suffers such restriction of movement.

But still to blame the PFA for acting 'more like an advisory service than a trade union, particularly at club level' and for 'propping up system that benefits a footballers' aristocracy at the expense of the rest' is really to have the cake and some more. The ending of the maximum wage and the Eastham court case, such a popular cause for progressive politics at the time *and* in popular memory ever since, effectively revolutionized the union's position so that it *could* never again be like a blue- or white-collar trade union bargaining simply over wages and conditions. Like it or not, whoever led the organization, its role was radically changed from 1961 onwards. All *Foul* and the *Leveller*'s backing for footballers' new freedom campaign nearly twenty years on amounted to was much-needed rhetoric. The terrain the PFA was fighting on was entirely different from the traditional conditions of the football industry in the 1950s, though at least public opinion was on the players' side to a greater degree in that decade.

Just how necessary the brief interventions of football's radical press were in the 1970s was highlighted by another short-lived publication, this time for the 1980s, *Football Kick!* The yuppies' revenge on *Foul*, the *Leveller* and the rest was glossy, 'adult-oriented' (that is it featured colour pics of semi-nude female models adorned in football kit) and complete with sharply right-wing editorials. A real footballing *Penthouse*. The self-proclaimed 'Greatest Ever Football Magazine' for 'grown-ups' was already, by issue 8, in November 1982 calling for the Thatcher government to implement its 'law and order' policies in the arena of football (and player) hooliganism and carried ex-Arsenal and Leicester City star Frank McLintock's trip down memory lane as he recalled from his Glasgow youth a certain Judge Carmont who was fond of dishing out sixteen-year jail sentences at the drop of a razor. In Big Frank's view Thatcher's hooligan problem would soon be over if the methods of the man who 'put the skids under the Scottish slashers' were adopted! Who needed the

The yuppies' revenge on Foul

Sun when *Football Kick!* was on the bookstalls?

Football's star treatment of players – their favourite colour, car, wife etc. – so beloved of football programme editors has had no systematic exploitation in the 1980s as, say, pop music has had in the form of *Smash Hits*. The *Face*'s younger sibling *The Hit* featured star strikers in hi-tech poses whilst the 'new' versions of long standing weeklies like *Shoot* and

Jimmy Greaves, Spurs and England

Match attempt a style format without really knowing what it is. What *Foul* had going for it was essentially its 'traditional' style and themes. It read like a Stan Bowles virtuoso performance – if it was published any later it would have carried 'tricky' Mickey Thomas's wink at the cameras (relayed for millions of viewers each weekend on television credits) after an opponent's 'foul' tackle. No postmodern journal has emerged to unsettle football and footballers in the 1980s though *Soccer International* still contrived to look bizarrely like a special issue of *Harpers and Queen*. In the television and video age this absence of a sense of critical humour from football's printed word leaves the 'field' for

the 'Saint and Greavsie' to ridicule Scottish goalkeepers and Hamilton Academicals till the cows come home and to practise their own brand of nostalgia for the age when they joined the ranks of the professional footballer – you guessed it, in the 1950s.

Off the box

For over half the 1985-6 season there was no coverage of League soccer on television, live or highlights: off the box for the first time since 1962. Ever since the beginning of the modern era the same debates have raged: how much 'live', how many action replays, how much analysis by 'experts'? When Blackpool played Bolton Wanderers on a Saturday night in the early 1960s for a television experiment, (two 'great' teams of traditional times performing the last rites of a Golden Age – black and white reactionaries waiting for 'colour' to signal their decline) the scene was set for the creation of a generation of armchair fans. Millions of enthusiasts, lectured by Jimmy Hill and Bob Wilson, were to have their introduction to football 'history' through television. Until the failure of Football League negotiators to wheel and deal in the mid-1980s, so that for instance no one was able to glimpse West Ham's one-man Denis Law revival show, Frank McAvennie, in his club colours unless they actually went to a match, television constantly cut up and pasted back together football's past. In the 1950s what is now the most important carrier of soccer nostalgia was just a glint in television programmers' eyes, and many of football's bosses at club and administrative level, would dearly like to return us there. No televized football, regionalization of the lower Leagues: a return to (effectively) a maximum wage system; sound like 1950s style all over again. Back to the future and 'real' football?

Jimmy Hill, ITV and BBC

What has also been a motivating force for the traditionalists is the 'ambivalence' of television towards football's 'problems' – hooliganism on and off the field. Plenty of players have felt the effect of trial by Jimmy Hill – trying to explain the context of what looks like a murderous foul or a gratuitous punch-up on a Monday morning to inquisitive fans after 'Match of the Day' replay machines have proved your guilt beyond a shadow of a doubt isn't always easy – and fans developed their own idiosyncratic answer to the television football focus on violence off the pitch. Hence 'Who the fuck is Jimmy Hill?' rang out loud and clear every time there was an unmissable 'incident', playing or spectating, in front of the cameras. What better calling card than a television slot in the homes of millions to remind other teams/fans/crews going green with envy: 'are you watching . . . ?' Everybody *was* watching when Liverpool beat Juventus *before* the European Cup Final of 1985 at the Heysel stadium in Brussels and television – however 'shocked' – revelled in it. The game as a 'spectacle' could never live up to this for 'incident', 'drama', 'controversy', a generalized 'newsworthiness' with plenty of 'talking points' for the panel in the studio and in the commentary box. This was *Rollerball* in the flesh: pre-match entertainment to knock 'Abide With Me' off the screens and sound mikes for ever. As a result of Heysel, Liverpool's 'proud reputation' as a 'hard' team to beat was firmly established, commanding 'respect' in Europe and in the football world at large. 'Are you watching, Barcelona?'! The team itself performed stoutly enough but there was little flair – there hadn't

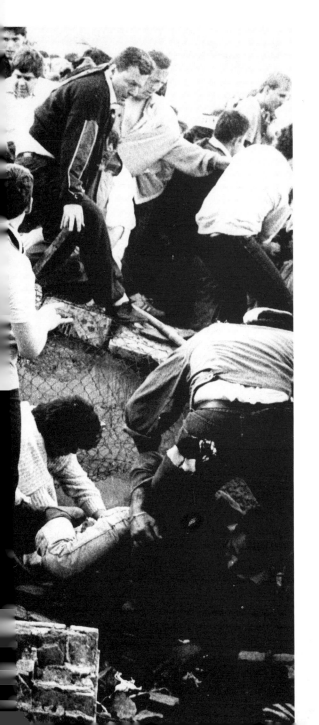

Heysel 1985

been much all season, 'hardman' Graeme Souness being difficult to replace – and the stylish Italian champions gained deserved 'revenge' easily enough when the match itself was played.

The effect of the global television and sundry media coverage of Heysel has been to lower the exchange value of televised football as never before. Football club secretaries and their chairmen were sent scurrying for their sepia snaps of football in the 1950s to remind the waiting journalists that one policeman and his dog were able to control 'large' football crowds without any trouble and not even have to help the referee out with player discipline. Or even early television footage from the beginning of 'Match of the Day' with scousers singing 'ditties' from the charts whilst Ian St. John dived to head in a Peter Thompson cross at the far post. Bring back Kenneth Wolstenholme, all is forgiven. It *was* colour television, flower power, student unrest and the ending of the maximum wage which started us on the road to ruin as they always said it would: players without earrings, hard work and no television coverage never did football any harm. Paranoia amongst club officials in 1985 set in so deeply that television programme makers were rudely rebuffed when they inquired about the possibility of filming at football grounds. The Football League started to require, in writing, a promise that no 'unsavoury' chants or incidents would be televised if film crews were allowed. Some clubs even denied that their fans sang anymore, or at all (Man. United among them!), and everyone had their eye on magistrates' decisions under the government's new law, *The*

Sporting Events (Control of Alcohol Etc) Act 1985, which would determine whether individual clubs were exempt from drink bans. Can you hear us off the box?

In fact, of course – or in television fiction – there will be no going back, no simple, traditional return to the 'natural', 'authentic', 'real' football played by real men. That particular section of the British population that gravitated towards professional football in the 1950s had already got sick and tired of the 'deferential workers' image and though grateful to get a game every week wanted something more out of the increasingly affluent, consumer society which was coming up around the bend. Television was an integral part of the end of wartime austerity in the 1950s. Man. United fans, in an emergency like not having a ground due to bombing, might just have stomached having to play home matches at Maine Road – even if it meant being part of crowds occasionally exceeding 70,000 or 80,000. But as the 1940s faded into the 1950s, as the age of 'austerity' got trampled by the age of 'affluence', as the Munich disaster came and went, they'd rather watch the game on the television (or on closed circuit tv) any day than swallow their pride and play on enemy turf at 'home'. Soon the good old days really existed only on videotape or in confused memories: an era was over when a 'historic' manager was scrapped to make way for modern methods and a new look. As Martin Hall wrote in *The Stan Cullis Blues*:

> the night Stan Cullis got the sack
> Wolverhampton wandered round in circles
> like a disallowed goal
> looking for a friendly linesman

For some, Wolves for example, there were to be no friendly officials and the long and winding road to bankruptcy petitions and the High Court was already being built. 'Old gold' would soon sound more like a new shipment of hash than Major Buckley's team colours at Molyneux. And, as Derek Dougan was about to find, old 'traditional' footballers never die – they survive enough of the modern era as they can stick and go on the telly, only to be tempted by the football industry once more and try to set up football clubs as 'workers co-ops'. But somebody had moved the goalposts since the 1950s and the modernists were well and truly in charge. Nobody told the traditionalists there'd be days like these. ■

3

Going bust, going bust, going bust

" Things are really bad – this is the only sponsorship we could get this season."

If football styles are in some way fighting back against the tombstone of nostalgia in modern soccer, the cards are still stacked against any sort of return to the 1950s, pure and simple. When the crunch comes, Cloggers United rool all in today's climate and the iron laws of relegation (as well as of economics) are ever ready to strangle the life out of ball players who dare to display their wares at a Saturday afternoon matinee. But it is football's financial crisis which has gripped the imagination of press, public and government in the 'free market' 1980s. Its glaring inequalities and public relations blind spots – which reportedly so 'shocked' the Prime Minister; £1 million transfers on top players, yet next to nothing on facilities for ordinary fans – only serve to highlight its lemming-like rush for the edge. The chant of 'Going bust, going bust, going bust' when taunting the team that made the previous week's bankruptcy story is increasingly being met by the ironic 'So are we, so are we' on rival terraces. I've lost count of the number of press 'investigations', television and radio documentaries in this decade focusing on football's 'crisis', carrying such startlingly original titles as 'Playing for Time', 'Time For a Penalty' and so on. Players, consciously or not, seem to be bound up in the process of giving 'value for money' as never before – work-rate, non-stop running all over the pitch, playing when they're seriously injured, even striving for 'entertainment'. Managers, however much they treat their players as robots, are at pains to shed the old image of negative, defensive football which so characterized the late 1960s and 1970s. All part of getting the product right. Like 'Top of the Pops' rather than 'The Tube', with a dash of Jimmy Greaves – modernism plus the wrapping paper. It may not bring the hordes back from the supermarkets and the do-it-yourself stores in time to watch the match before they go down the leisure centre, but at least they can say they've tried. The product, anodyne and anaesthetized, is now more than ever the thing: only, traditional virtues are to be resurrected at the expense of the modern vices that have crept in so pervasively over the last twenty years.

Team and individual soccer styles can only be part of this reconstruction of the fables of the football world: ground architecture, the game's industrial relations, the ownership and control of the clubs are all subject to the need for a purified modernity. A leaner, more healthy industry with 'real' jobs for the 'boys' who can keep their heads down and their mouths shut. Stadia that make sure people 'know their place': the playing field for players and the stands and terraces for spectators. Most of all, management of both clubs and teams by men who were born to run an enterprise and who know how to bat for Britain. Out of the ashes of the fire at Bradford City's Valley Parade will come a new footballing phoenix – souped-up and Super-Leagued – ready to fly the flag and speaking volumes for the economic recovery just around the corner. Or so we're told.

On the defensive

The Professional Footballers Association telegraphic address is 'Defensive Manchester', ominous not only for devotees of Maine Road – or even Old Trafford – but for a couple of thousand professional footballers as well. The union is still 'called in' by League, Association and club bosses to crisis meetings in the 1980s as if it was an unwanted newcomer on the subs bench about to be sent on loan to a club in the sticks. Yet its influence in these troubled times has grown so imperceptibly that by the time the 'big five' – Man. United, Spurs, Arsenal, Everton, Liverpool – were said to be breaking away to form a Super League in the 1985-6 season,

Gordon Taylor, the secretary to the PFA, was in some ways as important a figure in the negotiations as Ted Croker, secretary of the FA. Taylor's capacity to represent the vast majority of his membership in an industry with rapidly declining employment prospects meant that he could raise the spectre of a players' strike when the chips were down.

The image of the PFA as 'bosses' lackey' is one which has been periodically fuelled since the 1950s. Eamon Dunphy launched a vitriolic attack in the early 1970s which *Foul* published under the title of 'Part of the Union, Or The Mill Owner's Charter', arguing passionately that:

Eamon Dunphy, Millwall 1971

> The image of the Professional Footballer as a glamorous show-business type surrounded by pretty girls and flash cars is firmly implanted in most people's minds. I know him more accurately as the deeply insecure family man or the tearful failed Apprentice. Getting that image across is what the Professional Footballers Association, the players union, should be all about.
>
> And while it is often said that the Trade Union movement in Britain is too powerful, the equation between Union and power in football contains an element of black comedy.
>
> The PFA is a small organisation comprising two fulltime officials and fifteen hundred largely apathetic members. We have, in fact, practically no say in the game's decision-making process, there is no consultation process, and very little consideration of the players' point of view. It is a situation no normal Trade Union or professional body would tolerate for a moment.
>
> Consequently, our conditions of employment are such that a reincarnated nine-

teenth century mill owner would be gratified to see that restrictive practices so dear to his heart are alive and well in football.

Men can still be bought and sold in the market place, apprentices (*sic*) are callously dismissed on completion of their apprenticeship, and the possibility of retirement through injury, without compensation, looms over every game – an additional tension in an already high-risk profession.

The existence of such conditions could be regarded as a massive indictment of the PFA. However, this would be an over-simplification.

Derek Dougan

The object of Dunphy's derision was as much the 'apathy that exists among the superstars' as Cliff Lloyd, the players' union long-serving secretary at the time. Indeed, it was Lloyd's 'rare dedication' and (in combination with Jimmy Hill) his 'inspired leadership' which, according to Dunphy, overcame an 'apathetic membership' and 'relentless bosses' in the struggle to end soccer 'slavery' in the early 1960s. But the impression still lingered that if only 'wide boys' like Derek Dougan would stop using the union as a (self-) publicity machine a real labour-movement organisation could be built, with a properly class-conscious membership. Dougan's own reply to Dunphy's state-of-the-union message at the beginning of the 1973-4 season staunchly defended the union's 'softly, softly' approach since the mid-1960s. It rejected the accusation that the union was dragging its feet and listed its achievements in the field of wages and conditions and of disciplinary procedures up to that point. It also expressed the desire to fulfil the goals of freedom of contract and footballers' pension schemes, which were, in the late 1970s, to be the linchpin of a renewed groundswell of grassroots membership support for the union leadership in the 1980s of Alan Gowling and Steve Coppell.

After Derek Dougan's departure in the late 1970s, the age of flamboyant leaders, whether 'militant' or 'moderate' (Guthrie or Dougan) seemed to be well and truly buried. When Jimmy Guthrie bowed out in 1957, whether to the shouts of triumph from those who engineered a backroom coup as he alleged, or to the sighs of relief from a dissatisfied committee, a much more smart set stepped into the breach. The likes of Jimmy Hill, Noel Cantwell, Terry Neill, who became chairmen when the 'affluent footballer' was being born, eclipsed the image of the 'footballer as trade unionist' cloth-capping his way to the picket line outside the main gates of the ground. However mythical, the age of Guthrie, Charlie Roberts and Billy Meredith withered and died when chairmen who were silver-tongued and made-for-television came onto the scene.

Dougan represented a curious mixture of the working-class (Northern Irish) hero made bad – rebel on the field, but with a lust for television appearances. He combined the militant 'rhetoric' of a Jimmy Guthrie with the gift-of-the-gab of a Jimmy Hill. His departure from the PFA made way for a more self-consciously articulate, more highly educated grouping which too many observers mistook as simply middle-class and elitist, inheriting the tradition of white-collar football unionism.

The union men of the late 1970s and early 1980s were less dependent on cult figures who simply aspired to better club management – like Hill in the early 1960s with his Harold Wilson-style revolution at Coventry City or Dougan in the 1970s and 1980s at Kettering and Wolves. They have shown an acute awareness of the difficulties faced by a union so subject to Football League finance and patronage. Their background in higher education contradicts the Bob

Paisley 'humble' origins theory of football history encapsulated in the phrase 'we don't have many University lads here' – what Brian Hall and Steve Heighway, often publicized in the media as the 'brains' behind Liverpool's 1970s successes, thought about this retort to a journalist's question isn't recorded! But it also helps to make them a lot less prone to deference in negotiations with club, League and Association management at whatever level and less prepared to perpetuate the overweaning football disciplinary procedures whether the duty is for club or country.

Alan Gowling, one of the chairmen of the PFA in the post-1978 freedom of contract era, had his MA thesis for Manchester University banned from publication by the Football Association because it was thought to be – wait for it – 'disparaging to footballers'. Though later in the 1970s snatches of it were included in much-edited form in his 'pop' autobiography *Football Inside Out*, an example of the kind of material which Ted Croker and the rest of the old guard at Lancaster Gate took exception to was a quote from one player (who appeared in the thesis anonymously) having the gall to say that 'the club will shit on you if you let them'!

The PFA's 'moderate', even conservative, style has undoubtedly undermined images of the 'thick' but 'flash' footballer. In the years after Dougan, press concentration on the 'academic', 'sober', 'dull', defensive style of the PFA is in explicit contrast to its general football coverage, usually just a few column inches below. Paul Hince, an ex-professional player himself, and scourge of 'greedy' footballers ever since, welcomed Gordon Taylor's move to full-time secretary of the PFA after Cliff Lloyd's retirement with the headline 'Soccer's New Thinker'. Hince's news column went on:

> Although he is far too modest ever to admit it, Gordon Taylor is living proof that not all footballers carry their brains around in their boots.
>
> Educated to degree level, he is extremely articulate, with enough grey matter, one suspects, to walk into any job he sets his sights on.

Thatcher's flagship of Fleet Street, the *Daily Mail*, however, also took some comfort that 'polite' Cliff Lloyd would be succeeded by a man 'at least' having 'a grammar school education, O and A levels and, at his parents' insistence . . . embarked on a university course that eventually brought him a BSc in economics'.

What mattered though was that 'humble', 'deferential' and 'working-class' unionism in football was seen to be a thing of the past. Lloyd's departure from the PFA offices at Hanging Ditch in Manchester in 1981 after twenty-eight years as secretary, and the initiator of the change of name from 'union' to 'association' (because it 'abbreviated better and was more in keeping with the standing of members') symbolized this change in a nutshell. Lloyd had given up his job driving a scooter round a cable factory at Helsby, Cheshire, to join Liverpool as a wing half in 1937 and he later played for Fulham and Bristol Rovers before taking over from another dedicated secretary (and before that chairman) of the union, Jimmy Fay – a man seen by Jimmy Guthrie as 'a devoted Conservative'.

The Gowling, Coppell, Taylor era at the PFA puts paid to a whole mythology of the player as manual worker which, when taken to extremes,

Gordon Taylor

resembles Eastern bloc-style celebration of proletarian physical culture. Despite an early
twentieth-century legal ruling that a 'professional footballer was a manual labourer' the
soccer player has *never* simply been an employee
in any conventional sense. The difference between labour and pleasure for the professional
footballer is the bohemian one of not being at
'work'. That is quite apart from very specific
conditions of employment: as Lloyd pointed out
at the time of his retirement, they are virtually
the 'only professional people who have to retire
at around 35 years of age, the point at which
other professional men expect to go from
strength to strength . . . or did before the recession'. As Arthur Hopcraft said of Stan Cullis,
one of the major players of the 1930s who went
on to become one of the three or four leading
managers of the 1950s:

> He had moved out of the rigid oppressive-
> ness of his class through his gift in the
> people's art. The essence of the people's ob-
> session with football was that it was far,
> far better than work.

Minus its romanticism, this captures precisely
the aspect of professional football that the union
faces daily: the point where young, male, working-class dreams run up against the fiercely
autocratic regimes of football club culture and
end up as 'slaves' to the 'boss'. It may be far, far
better than 'work' but it sure ain't much fun
either.

In fact the union of Gordon Taylor and Mickey
Burns (as Further Education Officer) has,
against this backcloth, in the deepest economic
recession since the 1930s, miraculously managed to write the players' organization into the
record books. Derek Dougan and Percy Young
claimed (in *On The Spot*) that the 'classic' history of association football, edited by A.H.

Fabian and Geoffrey Green, only mentioned the
players' union twice in four volumes. This is not
entirely accurate – there are at least two other
references! – but mighty close. In a hostile environment and despite its somewhat contradic-
tory fight *both* for freedom of contract and for an
embargo on 'free trade' in 'foreign' footballers,
the PFA under Gordon Taylor has achieved mi-
leage without help from any other source and
relatively low subscription rates.

Where the union's road from serfdom will lead
is another question, though. In the face of
weekly scare-stories – real and unfounded – the
PFA has certainly managed to reactivate a
membership decimated by redundancies in the
1980s. It has 'sold' its services well in a market
where it has to compete with the advertising
bonanza open to a select few players, and with
the increase in power of agents in the sports industry generally. Perhaps a measure of this is
how often agents contact the PFA first – money-
to-burn players who use them should take note!
But just because a 'new' PFA has eclipsed the
traditional, deferential one of Fay, Lloyd and
others, it doesn't mean that it is all mod cons.
The workhorse mentality of a Brian Talbot –
running through the proverbial brick wall for
you – is still very much around and would have
done as an epitaph for League football, and its
politics, in any era. The union in 1980s football
means not much pop and only a snatch of style.

On the defensive but desperate as hell for a
new, more pleasurable, post-modern moment in
football culture, the PFA started the 1980s
under Alan Gowling's chairmanship wanting an
end to the infamous 'professional foul' – as

witnessed at Wembley in the 1980 FA Cup Final when Arsenal's Willie Young hacked down West Ham's Paul Allen. Under news headlines of 'PFA Seek Deterrent' the union was praised for its November 1980 suggestion that cynical tackles from behind should receive an eight-point penalty but it was really part of an early recognition by players in the 1980s that a certain flair and style needed to be reintroduced for the professional game to survive. As it turned out, just like the recommendation on the 'professional foul' itself, the union found too many deaf ears turned towards them until it was too late. The club chairmen's belief that it should be a sending-off offence carried the day in a law-and-order climate, followed by absurd refereeing decisions whilst the panic reigned the following season. As far as style in general was concerned on the football field, rather different conditions were looming to rescue the union's decision from the suggestion box.

The (top) people's game show

Professional football has always been a top people's game even if the majority of professionals are drawn from the lower orders. The 'people' in the people's game has also nearly always meant *males* whether from the top or bottom or middle of the social scale. Initially, in the late nineteenth century, as Tony Mason's social history *Association Football and English Society* (from 1863 to the First World War) shows, the professional game was watched largely by white, skilled working-class males. In the 1880s and 1890s the sport was administered by enthusiastic amateurs: both at the FA itself and, until the Northern teams with Scottish, Welsh and Irish 'cracks' (nineteenth-century jargon for 'superstar') took over, on the field. The Football League soon emerged to outrun the FA into the twentieth century, a rising

bunch of upstarts against the old aristocracy, and both combined to put down, until the modern era, any sustained attempt at trade-union organization. Though horse racing and polo might be more to royal taste the notion that there was about to be a working-class, players' coup in the club boardrooms has always been sheer fantasy.

Nowhere in modern industrial life since the turn of the century has there been more sustained paternalism than in the football business, nowhere more raw discipline, yet nowhere more opportunity (over the ninety minutes) to have some effect on the product that is consumed. Not a lot, but enough: freedom to make a bad pass (even though you might get a brown envelope with a demand for payment of a fine to the manager for breach of club discipline when you walk into the dressing room at half-time); or freedom to make a gesture to the stand or terrace (even if you might get your collar felt or your cards from the club secretary the next day). That's entertainment! Football's tales of the unexpected. All of the debates about who owns what in the football industry miss this essential point. What also counts is that, for the duration of the game at least, there is no complete control; in soccer everyone can be famous for a split second.

The campaigns to uphold wage restraint, the retain and transfer system and all the disciplinary paraphernalia that has surrounded the professional footballer since his birth in the 1870s, and legalization in the 1880s, have continued through to the present. Even when the shackles and chains of soccer slavery were partially severed the same prejudices fuelled the passions of those in charge. The mass media and football bosses delight in citing the union battles for contractual 'freedom' as the *cause* of the game's bankruptcy, stylistic and economic. Not for the first time the professional player in the

1980s is the natural scapegoat, whatever his earnings, prospects and potential. Eighty years ago, as it is today, football was about acknowledging your position. Professional footballers didn't always know their place; still don't. An article published in 1904 bemoaned the:

> Great pressure which . . . has been put on the London Football Association to admit professionalism, in order to meet the growing metropolitan demand for attractive 'football entertainments'. A natural distaste for the sordid business connected with commercial troupes, with registrations, wages, riotous assaults and deliberate foul play has long made the officials of the LFA hesitate. Men who play for recreation's sake will not enjoy settling the wrangles of those who work for an obviously financial motive.

The anonymous writer went on to press home 'the-money-is-the-root-of-all-evil' theme with an attack on the Americanization of sport and declining moral values:

> If the professional Englishman is at present alone in his proud possession of the 'international foul', it has also remained for an English team, beaten on the field, to claim a victory on some technical flaw in their opponents' correspondence. Many other results flow from the gradual abolition of any difference between those business proceedings on which a man's livelihood depends and the purely recreative features of a pastime which contributes nothing to a balance-sheet . . . [T]he process can be neatly paralleled across the Atlantic. The winning of a game being the only end that an American player has in view, he subordinates every other consideration to this and cheerfully relinquishes such old-fashioned ideals as 'style' or 'good form', or the other shibboleths which have become antiquated in the land of their birth, and are scarcely known at all in newer countries . . . But our players have an even greater incentive to success than the American's thirst for victory. Our professionals' bread and butter – or shall we say their grouse and claret? – depend upon their doing well in the league games and the cup ties. So we deliberately try to maim our opponents as early as possible in the year's contest, and shout for protective legislation if we find that the frank, old-fashioned charge is likely to bring disablement upon ourselves. During the first week in last September no time was lost in the match between Blackburn Rovers and Bury. McClure, a centre half, was ordered off the field at Ewood Park for intentionally damaging an opponent, who had to be assisted to the pavilion. His side were not beaten, though they finished with only nine players, for Birchall had his face split open. It was a pleasant beginning of the season . . . [O]n the whole, it will probably be admitted that . . . football is not an asset of which we can be justly proud, and that its main faults have arisen through the prominence of pecuniary considerations which its ruling association has of late so strikingly endorsed.

That 'lower-class players' could achieve the status of highly-paid athletes and, worse, that a

Malcolm Allison

John Bona

man could 'fix his own price' caused seething discontent in the late nineteenth century. Just as it does in our time. Warnings, so familiar nowadays, were given that the men 'who, towards the end of the [eighteen] eighties, headed the movement and fought the first battles for professionalism never realised how far the system would go' and players' 'big salaries' were frequently put up as the root of more than merely moral bankruptcy. As one leading amateur wrote in 1894:

> There are rumours of much bankruptcy in the air and lately we read in a football paper of a club that had to part with its players very cheaply . . . The professional is an expensive luxury . . .

Sounds like the *Times* in the mid-1980s!

Meanwhile, back in the dug-out, managers rattle their watch chains and trot out the usual forms of petty disciplinary regulation as if players are naughty schoolboys not wearing their required blazers. Indeed, absence of required blazers is precisely the sort of action club fines are levied for. The surest truism in football is that the boss is the 'boss'. As John Bond told millions of television viewers, and his new charges at Man. City, in a Granada documentary on the failure of the second coming of Malcolm Allison to Maine Road:

> While you're here I'd like to think that you and I will know each other, I'll know you as the players and you'll know me as 'boss'. I don't say that for any other reason – for me to be the boss because I want to be up there and you to be down there – but I think it's absolutely right because I think it shows a mark of respect . . . from now on in, when we're together you'll know me as 'boss'.

Bond then went on to describe the 'little forms of discipline' that were to be instituted in his reign at the club in the early 1980s:

> If people misbehave and do things wrong
> . . . for instance, if you're late in training
> you get fined; if you're late for the coach,
> you get fined; on match days everybody . . .
> will wear a collar and tie and jacket . . .
> That will be done, if you don't do that you'll
> be fined.

Perhaps it was with some justice that Bond – all blow-dried hair, flash leather jacket and gold bangles – was the manager of Swansea City when they went to the brink at the end of 1985 just three years after leading the First division. He spent his last days as 'boss' of the 'bombed' club – another case of failed in Wales – moaning that the local council had refused to find £200,000 to bail out the dying Swans when it was always forking out for 'piddling little minority projects'.

Disciplinary machinery *has* improved, so that players have some means of redress when bosses are on the ball, but not much. In Derek Dougan's handy guide *How Not To Run Football* (complete with bad taste cover, George Best being crucified on a cross surrounded by 'hooligan' fans whilst pound notes swirl around Wembley's twin towers) he recalls the PFA's success in improving players' rights in the 1970s:

> Until 1973 disciplinary procedures in the
> game caused a great deal of heartburn.
> The 'courts' run by the FA were often no
> more than the 'kangaroo' variety. Justice
> was not always done, nor seen to be done.
> Players were resentful, feeling they would
> not get a fair hearing and referees were
> uncomfortable appearing before the dis-
> ciplinary committees to give evidence.
>   Hearings were often reduced to fiascos,
> when players felt the evidence was loaded
> against them and that an official's word
> would always be preferred to theirs. Inde-
> pendent witnesses were not allowed, as I
> found to my cost when I appeared before a
> committee during my time with Wolves.
>   After patient and constructive nego-
> tiations between the PFA and the Football
> Association, new procedures were worked
> out . . . The result is that we now have a
> system light years ahead of that which
> applied until the early 1970s.

True, progress has been made but like everything in the workings of the football industry only slowly and unevenly. The totting up points system which now applies – automatic bans or fines, with no right of appeal, once certain disciplinary point levels are reached – is heavily dependent on arbitrary interpretations of the laws of the game by unpredictable referees. Club fines are meted out by dictatorial management, occasionally with the help of senior players. Charges of bringing the game into disrepute are notoriously controversial though video evidence can mitigate immediate harshness. What it still boils down to is rigorous enforcement of petty rules by tyrannical overlords: managers, directors, administrators. Ask Justin Fashanu about Labour-voting Brian Clough when he tried to train at the City Ground whilst officially banned! A Thatcherite dreamworld in fact: a model for the rest of industry (what's left of it in football's major centres) to follow. A world where players play and bosses boss. All sheepskin coats and BMWs. Derek Hatton always did look more like an up and coming midfield player than a labour leader, and – as *The Face* christened him – DaDoo RonRon Atkinson has done almost as much for menswear and expensive

DaDoo RonRon
Atkinson

Valley Parade, 1985

Foiled attempt to ban
Scottish fans,
Wembley 1981

male jewellery as the Casuals. Football, bankruptcy style!

After the fire this time

If the player – as workers are generally – is the
favourite target for blame during the whole history of the football industry's crisis (that is from
day one in the late nineteenth century) the
archaic financial and architectural settings of it
are not far behind. When part of Bradford City's
ground went down in May 1985 it was an apt
symbol of the death of traditional and, in some
ways, modern football. When Margaret
Thatcher stood in its ruins with club chairman,
Stafford Heginbotham, posing with char-
acteristic 'social concern' for the photographers
(stand down, Margaret?!) it was also an app-
ropriate comment on national decline. The condition and safety of football grounds in England
and Wales (and Scotland and Northern Ireland
for that matter) neatly reflects the death of
manufacturing Britain, the de-industrialisation
of a kingdom, better than any other urban land-
scape. 'Bradford's burning' conjures all sorts of
racial and political tension for the popular press
but the neglected, decaying, wooden stand of
Valley Parade really said it all. Bradford Park
Avenue had already gone the way of all glorious
club pasts over a decade before, a prelude of
what was to come for Bradford and many other
manufacturing towns. The fire next time looks
likely to be the decimation of League football as
it has become known and several hundred more
players on the dole unless the PFA can mobilize
a rearguard action as never before. Part-time
football has been accepted for many years, in
any case, as a base for the union to start its fight-

back strategy and regionalization is probably an inevitable corollary. A casual workforce for a decentralized country – what better sign of the times for the 1980s in Thatcher's Britain?

Very few football clubs have ever been models of profitable businesses. But the 1980s are witnessing an unprecedented commercialization of soccer aimed at 'modernizing' the game's image and raising the status of its consumers. The massive increases in executive boxes, hit temporarily by the government's legislation to ban alcohol in the summer of 1985, is one clear illustration of soccer's appeal for more 'respectable', business-oriented client-customers. Share flotations in the City and massive sponsorship deals with people who wouldn't know a back pass from an underpass are seen by the big clubs as a means of going back to the brief period of commercial success in the early post-war period. Most clubs have long since given up relying simply on gate money, so running pools and other schemes have been essential to keep the remaining generous local bank managers from the players' entrance. But the restructuring of football capital now manifestly taking place is still likely to take these smaller clubs down the road apiece to closure. 'We Are The Champions' b/w 'Another One Bites The Dust', with grateful thanks to Freddie Mercury!

Football's split into many poor and a few rich clubs is increasingly compounded by the stress on international competition and the need for the major sides (and occasionally the small fry) to travel in Europe. The Football League's panic response to the UEFA ban on English clubs after the Heysel disaster in May 1985 was to introduce a Super Cup (sponsored by Screen Sport: a sign of things to come in soccer – video, video) to fill the fixture gap for the clubs who were banned. On top of that a Full Members Cup, organized initially on a regional basis, was instituted. That was with the Freight Rover Trophy for lower division clubs already in existence plus the usual overkill fixture list nightmares of League, 'Milk' Cup and FA Cup games. English soccer's team styles are moulded by such madness – super-fit machine-men who in the end just start going through the motions – and eventually even the crowds have got wise. The wrangles over television payment for coverage of 'live' and recorded soccer highlights in the 1980s has finally led to Super League fantasies (like British Cup dreams, too) coming close to being translated into reality. Manoeuvres by some club chairmen in the 1985-6 season effectively laid down the ever-present threat of a breakaway League, whether sooner (in the 1980s) or later (in the 1990s). Change or we quit and play with our own ball is met meekly by 'hey, mister can we have our ball back?' on behalf of the Third, Fourth and, to some extent, Second division clubs.

There are plenty of takers when Liverpool, Everton, Arsenal, Spurs and Man. United are shaking the coffers: desperate 'big city' clubs like Man. City, Chelsea, West Ham, Newcastle, Sheffield Wednesday, Aston Villa and Nottingham Forest can't afford to look a gift horse in the mouth and their club secretaries' eyes are already glazing over with the prospects of money-spinning matches all across the United Kingdom. Regionalization of the Leagues (as existed last in the glorious 1950s when there was a North-South divide) plus, at the very least, a chopping back of the First division marks a prophetic step along the road towards football in the next century. Hi-tech top clubs whilst the rest flounder in the bankruptcy courts. A final killing of the sentimental in football (when Crewe Alexandra can look forward to *not* being beaten 13-2 by Spurs) just as we find in the national economic map with the decimation of the old manufacturing industries which the club depended on for their support.

The irony is that all the stress on fewer, bigger, better clubs playing increasingly across national borders or in regional competitions is placing emphasis precisely on the regional pride which so marks out 1980s football-watching; soccer's style wars, on the field and off depend on the rivalries between and within the localities which football clubs in diverse ways represent. 'We're the pride of . . .'/'You're the shite of . . .' reflect increasingly deep economic and social divisions. Our national past is being relived on the pitch and stands and terraces every week, but that past is based on notions of one nation/empire/commonwealth, which incorporates, however, a sense of English superiority over the Scots, Welsh and Irish. These contradictions are reflected when Northern Ireland, Scotland or Wales are close to qualifying for anything, or when only those countries' clubs are involved in Europe: suddenly they become 'ours' – surrogate English; overnight the jokes about Scottish goalkeepers, the 'luck' of the Irish, or the 'hard luck' of the Welsh aren't quite so funny any more.

Ignoring of the Chester Reports of 1968 and 1983 has meant a long drawn-out death for League football but will Super Leagues solve the problem of what to do with our leisure time? The mad and desperate scramble to be 'on top' is likely to continue for a couple of seasons yet but there is little doubt that the end is nigh. One hundred years is a *very* long time in football: by the 1980s 'trad' soccer with its complex of styles and cultural meanings is buried already beneath modern soccer's consumerist madhouse, but any postmodern era is likely to have a more flashy, packaged, expensive look to it, without any traditional 'heart'. 'Can you hear us *in* the box?' will be the 'likely lads' menacing chant! ∎

4 You'll never walk again

Football has always been a violent game. The modern era in professional soccer is no exception. Year in, year out numerous players sustain serious injuries from both deliberate and accidental fouls on the field. Since the modern age began there has also been a pronounced element of fan violence around football; by no means, necessarily, any worse than the 'hooliganism' accompanying soccer matches in the early years of the professional game in the last century, though certainly of a different form in the 1960s, 1970s, and 1980s.

In the 1984-5 season, however, there were a number of incidents at and around football grounds which were seen in many quarters as signifying the death of football as we know it: in May 1985 alone, a fire at Valley Parade, Bradford City's ground, destroyed one of the most antiquated stands in the Football League, killing 56 people and seriously injuring hundreds more. The man identified by police as leader of the Cambridge Casuals (the Main Firm), nicknamed the General, was sentenced to five years' imprisonment after allegedly organizing a militaristic attack on a visiting Chelsea crew; 'live' on television millions witnessed a series of charges by Liverpool and other English supporters at the Heysel stadium in Brussels before the European Cup Final against Juventus, which led to the collapse of parts of the ground and the deaths of 39 people and, again, serious injuries for hundreds of others.

Are these spheres of violence linked? Does, for instance, footballers' violence lead to football violence? The irony of Graeme Souness, football's best known hard man since Norman Hunter hung up his hatchet, commenting, as studio guest on BBC television, on the Brussels tragedy as it unfolded will live long in popular memory but is there any connection? The selfsame television audience can watch, weekly, as Football League referees allow cruel maiming

and deliberate kicking to go unpunished, whilst bookings and sendings-off for offences such as dissent and 'ungentlemanly conduct' are legion. Why, when the football authorities are crying out for the game to be cleaned up, put up with such a charade?

It's a man's, man's, man's game.

One of the justifications is football's need to perpetuate its 'macho' image. Watching professional soccer in the 1960s, 1970s and 1980s reveals a great deal about changing images of masculinity. Ted Croker, interviewed on an Open University television programme on *Women and Sport*, described to an astonished interviewer that one of the reasons women could not play football at the same level as men was because of the shape of their chests, which males in time-honoured fashion used to control the ball. Flat caps, rattles, long shorts, big boots *and* chest traps: the golden days of professional soccer when men were men and women stayed at home to wash the kit. No wonder the men who run football fought so hard in the law courts over Theresa Bennett's claim to be registered as a member of a boys' (amateur) soccer team and rejoiced when the judge decided, predictably, that football did not come within the Sex Discrimination Act 1975. Someone should send them all a video of Bill Forsyth's *Gregory's Girl* where girls playing football is described enthusiastically by the teenage male hero as 'modern'. Lord Kinnaird would have been proud of the traditionalism stoutly upheld by these bastions of male chauvinism, like Lord Denning who

Dee Hepburn in Gregory's Girl

declared, when hearing the case, that the law would be:

> exposing itself to absurdity . . . if it tried to make girls into boys so that they could play in a football league . . . football is a game [in] which the average woman is at a disadvantage to the average man because she has not got the stamina or physique to stand up to men [or] . . . the strength or the stamina to run, to kick or tackle.

Game, set and match to Ted Croker and his boys!

The 'kicking game' (as opposed to handling games like rugby) is often just that. Andy Gray, Everton's striker in their 1985 championship side and renowned for his aerial ability and bravery in situations where others fear to head, broke the nose of a Bayern Munich opponent in the European Cup Winners' Cup semi-final at Goodison Park in April 1985, sparking press comment that football was becoming ever more calculated and cynical in its old age. The *Guardian* ventured to suggest that in view of Gray's reputation for nutting the ball, *and* his opponents (often sustaining horrible facial injuries himself in the process), the incident was less than accidental. It could be seen as part of a general trend toward more systematic head and face injuries resulting from players deliberately going for headers in order to inflict severe damage on their opponent. Such incidents aren't, of course, always motivated by malice but doubt still surrounds clashes like the one where Kenny Dalglish fractured his cheekbone after a challenge from Kevin Moran, effectively shortening the Liverpool player-manager's career. Moran, similar to Gray in that they come joint top of the 'player-most-likely-to-require-stitches-in-his-own-face' league table, displays a footballing style more akin to Gaelic football,

Kevin Keegan scores against Scotland, 1979

which did in fact nurture him until he became a late recruit to professional soccer.

The increase of deliberate violence of this kind on the football field is connected to a generally more ruthless approach all round which has been gathering pace since the beginning of the modern era in the 1960s. 'Tough', 'hard', even 'dirty' have become familiar descriptions of both team and individual player styles for the last twenty years. By the early 1970s it was possible to appreciate the full force of what had been going on at some top clubs and at international level during the 1960s: runners were beginning to take over from skilful players on a widespread scale at every club. In short Keegan displaced Best as the footballer even the most cloistered judges should have heard of. At the end of the decade David Lacey wrote:

> The seventies has not produced another Best. Kevin Keegan, dedicated professional, keen family man, highly commercialised and articulate, is the typical international product of the age. Personally, however, one would willingly sacrifice five hours of Keegan for five minutes of Best at his peak.

The darker side of this development was that 'kickers' became institutionalized. The 1960s had its share of 'choppers' (Ron Harris at Chelsea, John McPhee at Blackpool, Nobby Stiles at Man. United). Jack Charlton received great publicity when, as Leeds United and England centre-half, he was reported to carry round a 'little black book' (literally or metaphorically, it hardly mattered) with the names of opponents in it who merited some kind of retributive justice. Charlton's club (and, occasionally, England) team-mate Norman Hunter made 'bite-your-legs' tackles into an art form. The fact that Hunter's brutal fouls failed to

Clive Thomas takes charge

overshadow what his fellow professionals constantly reminded us were hidden skills of the highest order (he was always a players' player) just goes to show the depth of tolerance within the game for cynical violence reached by the late 1960s.

When Peter Storey of Arsenal became an international under Alf Ramsey the twin developments, hard running and cool kicking, had come together with a vengeance. It was all dressed up, by coaches and the men from the media, in the language of 'professionalism' and 'character' but everybody knew what it meant. As a 1980s child of these parents, Graham Roberts of Spurs put it, much to *Private Eye's* glee: 'Football's a game of skill . . . we kicked them a bit and they kicked us a bit.'

Which is where the soccer version of the *Eye* came in. *Foul* highlighted these symptoms, documenting the antics of the class of 1966. But is it true to say that professional football has become dirtier or more violent and dangerous to play than it was, say, twenty, thirty or even a hundred years ago?

Clive Thomas, one of football's moralizing band of referees, has argued that 'football is not as hard, in the kicking sense, as it was'. The 1980s in other words are an improvement on the 1970s. But much has depended on the response of the authorities. As David Lacey noted in his long goodbye to the 1970s:

> the mood is not so harsh as it was. At the beginning of the 1971-2 season League referees were instructed to tighten up on the laws relating to fouls and misconduct, a laudable exercise spoilt to some extent by

82

the secretive way it was carried out. Even
so players now think twice before hacking
each other down from behind and there is a
breed of player brought up not to tackle
from behind at all.

Bobby Charlton, Gentleman Jim of English
football – Mr Clean – complained that during
the 1970s players were being pampered by referees and that a certain toughness had gone *out*
of the game. Not that he was advocating the
scything down of skilful footballers – which he
epitomized so well – but that football had lost a
degree of manliness, according to his touchline
judgement. Such a conception of masculinity
allowed Clive Thomas to bracket together some
rather odd 1960s bedfellows when he claimed, in
an interview, that:

> the Bremners, Hunters, Balls and even
> Bobby Charltons (because he could moan
> a bit) would accept authority whether
> they agreed with a decision or not. Today
> young players want to confront you at
> every turn.

No doubt this same conception of masculinity,
strong *and* obedient towards authority, was one
of the keenest sources of the much publicized
tension between Charlton and George Best in
their days together at Man. United. It is
somewhat ironic, for Charlton, that both flair
and violence are back in vogue in the football
world in the 1980s. Part of the philosophy behind the football authorities' campaign – another of their periodic panics, doomed as ever to
failure – to stamp out kissing and other forms of
celebration of a goal being scored is rooted in this
acute self-consciousness about where the
boundaries of masculinity really are. The most
recent crackdown on football's equivalent of
'gender-bending' came in the 1983-4 season, fol-

Bryan Robson

lowing a similar effort two years previously. Clive Thomas was again at the centre of controversy, intervening to stop West Ham players celebrating a goal against Man. United in a televized League game, but he was, like other referees who adopted similar poses, merely obeying orders. The desire to stamp out 'girlish' behaviour by male football players, to keep the spectacle an overwhelmingly masculine one, was only one of the themes behind such official interventions, but it reinforced the pervasive view that femininity has no place on the park: 'you woman', 'you big girl' are no idle terrace taunts, they simply reiterate the managers' half-time team talk. The fact that female footballers are stopped from progressing to the male professional arena by law and bureaucracy underlines the image of a man's game played and watched – as it always was in football mythology – by 'real' men. As Bryan Robson said, with a hint of sympathy for the less than masculine, flair players and perhaps foreseeing Uruguay's tactics in the 1986 World Cup in Mexico:

> They shout at each other. They swear at each other. They kick each other, too, which is worse. It's a rough game ... A rough game. I don't complain for myself – but when ball players like Gordon Strachan get kicked off the park it spoils the entertainment for the fans who come to see them perform.

A very low profile, especially in the sports pages of the Fleet Street comics, is given to violence on the field overall and particularly vendettas between individual players or even specific teams with old scores to settle. It is as if fouls are always 'professional', in the sense that they are deliberately committed to prevent an opponent scoring or gaining an advantage, or else they are only accidental, mistimed or clumsy challenges.

The story from within soccer's goldfish bowl is quite different. Scuffles, and much worse, take place frequently because of last season's dust-up or because a player's wife has gone off with someone else from the same club. Until recently, the nature of these incidents has frequently been hidden behind closed club doors or at least behind the oak panels of football's administration. When Aston Villa's former captain, Dennis Mortimer, then on loan to Sheffield United, was struck, off the ball, by Roger Wylde of Barnsley, an incident which necessitated six stitches in a lip wound, the action taken was merely to appeal to the Football Association in its capacity as a disciplinary commission. Mortimer himself stated after the verdict, which went against him only on the grounds of insufficient evidence: 'I shall not take it to a civil court. I wanted to keep this within the realms of our profession.'

However, the charge itself, 'insulting or improper behaviour or acting in a manner likely to bring the game into disrepute' was the first to be brought by a private complaint, one professional player against another.

Mortimer claimed that despite the decision:

> I felt I was justified in taking this case to the FA on a matter of principle and to clear up one or two aspects of our game which I feel should be highlighted. This season I've watched a lot of first division football when I have not been playing and there is a certain element coming into the game. Players are more determined to win and are more ruthless. We are all there earning a living and we want to do that for as long as we can. It is a game I have played for 16 years and one I love. But I feel it is becoming a dangerous sport to play because of the way teams are being geared up.

The *Times* reported Mortimer's case as a 'partial

victory' but it is clear that the Football Association, as so often, either couldn't, or else wouldn't, probe deeply enough to get to the bottom of the incident.

In some ways such cases make it more likely that players will follow the Scottish precedent set by Jim Brown, former international and Dunfermline Athletic captain, who sued for damages against John Pelosi of St Johnstone, whose foul tackle broke Brown's leg and ended his playing career. It was the first civil court case of its kind, involving a *professional* footballer and undoubtedly set £ signs lighting up in many players' eyes. The weekend that Brown's out of court settlement of £30,000 was reported in the press, Derrick Parker, then of Oldham, formerly of Barnsley, a club he had left in a hurry, was considering similar legal action against Barnsley's centre half at the time, Mick McCarthy. Nothing came of it in the end, suggesting that rumours of intrigue at Oakwell before Parker was transferred were correct, but next time the financial incentives of a successful trip to judges' chambers may be irresistible.

But has it not always been this way? In the 1950s the criminal law was always on hand, in the person of police officers; if an opposition player was sent off for violent conduct the manager of the player on the receiving end was asked if charges might be brought in the criminal courts. Furthermore, the history of the game is sprinkled with accounts of players being prosecuted, and sometimes convicted, for assaults on the field either against other players or involving spectators. It is more that by the 1980s the combination of a growing awareness of the possibilities of *both* civil and criminal liabilities for actions on the field, and a new zealousness about policing at football matches and around the grounds, has ensured a fresh panic about how far footballers can go in order to prove their manhood.

Dennis Mortimer

Bastards in black and boys in blue

The roughness of football culture has always been secondary to its respectability, its hob-nobbing with the rich and powerful. Only now, in the 1980s, is roughness seen as an irredeemable liability – there was uncertainty in previous eras which led to equivocation – which the game can do without. Working-class manners, downtown versions anyway, in leisure pursuits have long been the subject of regulation from above, from cock-fighting to spitting and swearing on the field of play in the last quarter of the twentieth century. Jimmy Greaves and Ian St John are by no means the only spitting images in modern football. Immortalized by *Not the Nine O'Clock News*'s 'Gob of the Month' feature, in slow motion action replay of course, such backstreet behaviour has begun to offend football's governing bodies, nervous about the (occasionally) watching politicians, dignitaries and 'respectable' potential television audience.

Referees have been at the sharp end of this changing concern though most of them have joyfully carried out their masters' bidding, fully conscious of the notoriety (always helpful for getting onto the after-dinner speaker circuit) which comes from a mention on the 'Jimmy Hill programme'. Referees like Gordon Hill, who used to win players' respect by swearing *back* at them, are few and far between. Now they are increasingly likely to be impressed by star status – some of the more controversial ones are indeed stars in their own right – which is reflected in their use of players' first names when refereeing top teams ('Take it easy, Norman', 'How's it going, Jimmy') hardly endearing themselves to lower-division nonentities or even the players in the First Division outside the big city clubs. The best referees are still the ones who nobody notices.

Televised games are a real temptation for the

Jimmy Greaves of TV–AM and the Saint and Greavsie show

men in the middle. The 1985 FA Cup Final saw referee Peter Willis (in the costly words of Jimmy Greaves) write his name into the history books by, to the utter disbelief of ninety-five per cent of the worldwide audience, sending off Kevin Moran for a late tackle on Everton's Peter Reid. Willis, who just happened to be a policeman with a reputation in the game for resolution and firmness which would go down a storm at a Tory party conference, had already provoked a near riot at Maine Road in a League game a fortnight earlier. He had sent off a Man. City player who called him a 'twat' after he had allowed play to go on long after a young colleague had been seriously injured by a late (and unpunished) tackle from an Oldham opponent. Willis had, as they say in the game, lost his bottle (though he nearly collected several more round his head as he left the pitch at half-time) and it was really no surprise when he confused Moran's challenge with a re-run of Willie Young's calculated tackle in the same arena during the FA Cup Final four years earlier. Such is the stuff of crowd trouble the back (and front) pages are so fond of saying comes directly from players' indiscipline on the field.

In truth, football authorities and governments of whatever shade have been much more interested in images of players as deferential workers at play. As long as they are not rocking any boats or disturbing the moral sensibilities of occasional television viewers, they can happily kick lumps out of whoever they like. The kickers will get away with their misdemeanours because that's just how they'll be treated: as less serious than indiscipline of the tongue and in-

Charlie George and friends

subordination by gesture or expression. The only time such strategy doesn't really come off is when there is collective rucking on the field involving numerous players from both sides. This is still relatively rare in English football – it remains one of the areas where 'foreign' football is shown in Saturday lunchtime highlights and offered up as contrasting unfavourably with the home product – though it may not be for long. Soccer is a remarkably individualistic game, for all its emphasis on team work and the modern era's distrust of flair players. Compared to ice-hockey or rugby or American football there are relatively few instances of mass player violence during and after games. Similarly collective solidarity off the pitch is hard to find though teams do occasionally go on strike (there has never actually been withdrawal of labour by League footballers *en masse* despite coming very close to it on a number of issues over the years) and even vent their collective frustration against club property together. Since the ending of the maximum wage, individual wage bargaining has further undermined the potential for collective action on conventional industrial grievances. On the field, players needing protection from the potential hard men of the opposing side usually rely on their own team's tough guys putting greater fear of God into anyone who might be contemplating over-the-ball maiming or off-the-ball mugging. Weakness – that is not wanting to start the kicking – is seen as the invitation to mete out whatever punishment the referee in question will tolerate.

It is really the police, as symbol of law-and-order society, rather than football's own figures of authority, referees, that have stepped purposefully onto the grass in the 1980s. Pitch invasions by our blue boys, whether to eject luckless television reporters trying to interview a player at the scene of the action, or, more seriously, to warn players that their routine Saturday afternoon match behaviour might constitute more than a bookable offence, have become increasingly common. When Sergeant Ruggles strode between Mel Blyth and his own goalkeeper on the day Millwall, rather more famous for its fighting crews than its players, went to Colchester in the 1980-1 season, it was not the first time a police invasion had stopped play. But the potential for such innovative refereeing is clearly much greater today than say in the 1960s when a similar incident occurred at Portsmouth. Not that central defenders like Mel Blyth (what he did to forwards on the pitch, Millwall's F-troop, Treatment and Bush-wackers have been practising elsewhere ever since) never swore at their own goalkeeper, or vice versa. Rather, a more strident police mentality has emerged, the kind which redefines shouting 'scab' on a picket line as criminal behaviour and regularly looks at the decadence on and off the field and simply *despairs*. Is it really accidental, though, that it was Charlie George, plucked from the North Bank and constantly labelled by the media and his various clubs as a 'tearaway', who was amongst the players prosecuted for on-the-field events in the early 1980s (or in Scotland that Davie Cooper, Rangers' 'temperamental' winger found himself before the Sherriff's court)? Flair and flare-ups seem to have gone hand in hand ever since George Best. Charlie George, when playing for Southampton at Norwich City in the same season as the Blyth incident, hit a press photographer at the side of the pitch and was later fined £400 for threatening behaviour likely to cause a breach of the peace. In a way, George's prosecution confirmed his reputation as a bad boy and underlined further his exclusion from the national side at an earlier stage of his career alongside other flair players who hadn't got quite the discipline and deference required – Peter Osgood, Stan Bowles, Alan Hudson and the rest of the gang.

'Incidents' on the field have frequently been perceived to be likely to spark off trouble on the terraces. Sammy Nelson and Terry Mancini's 'short droppings' have passed into football's folk-lore but they were regarded at the time as possible incitements to riot. The belief that players' violence or indiscipline *causes* football violence on the terraces, seats, public transport, pubs and shopping centres is becoming widespread. Journalists like Hugh McIlvanney and Arthur Hopcraft, in many respects the best of the genre, as well as more predictably the likes of Jeff Powell of the *Daily Mail* have at one time or another floated the idea. Powell went as far in 1980 as to say that: 'it is almost beyond argument now that violence on the pitch inflames trouble on the terraces.'

It's certainly true that there is a connection between what happens on the field and what happens in the stands or on the terraces, but the argument that there is a direct line from player violence or indiscipline to spectator violence or indiscipline is as silly as the other widely prop-agated myth that alcohol causes football viol-ence. Rather, as a correspondent to the *Guardian* letters page pointed out in the after-math of the Brussels tragedy, if the lads get tanked up it is to be able to better enjoy the trouble and mayhem.

The complex mixture of spectator/team em-otions is clearly evident in incidents like the much publicized Man. United crowd invasion in 1974 which caused the abandonment of their local derby with Man. City, leaving United rel-egated to the Second Division. Losing 1-0 with five minutes to go could be seen as a good en-

ough reason to go over the top. Similarly Not-tingham Forest fans' invasion at Newcastle, also in 1974, when their side were also losing, boosted their own players enough to resurrect the game and turn potential defeat into a 4-3 victory, only for the result to be declared void. Scorelines rather than body counts are more im-

*Sammy Nelson's
Arsenal*

worked up. Chants such as 'You're so bad it's unbelievable' and 'What the fuck is going on?' can
be preludes to pitch invasions just as much as
players kicking lumps out of each other.

Even so, professional football players' behaviour is now regulated by government, governing bodies and police *as if* it was a *direct*
cause of hooliganism as well as in and for itself.

Thatcher's boys

Blue and white, red and white and other 'barmy
armies' are for the colour supplements and pop
sociology papers the face of football followers
today. The rise of the Casuals has been noted
less for its association with style than trouble:
for example, on *Sport on 2* (Radio 2) in a documentary on football hooliganism in Scotland;
in the *Observer* magazine under the headline
'Saturday Afternoon Fever'; and, after the 'General' Leslie Muranyi trial, in the *Mirror*. Maxwell's mouthpiece proclaimed under the banner
headline 'Savages' that:

the evil mastermind of the Cambridge supporters' attack on Chelsea fans . . . ordered
them all to wear smart Pringle jumpers,
denims and training shoes to make them
look more like the boy next door than soccer hooligans. The Chelsea fans were
caught in pincer movements with all exits
cut off and trapped against a barricade.
The plan worked to horrifying and blood-
stained perfection and resulted in the
worst-ever street violence seen in Cambridge.

portant to terrace/pitch relations, especially in
the context of the season's progress, past rivalries, local derby hatreds and regional resentment. Team styles too frequently mean more
than isolated incidents. Boring, drab, defensive
performances week after week, or someone's
hilarious ineptitude get loyal supporters just as

New wave fans, Chelsea 1983

Judge Christopher Hilliard, sentencing Muranyi to jail, had told him: 'You are articulate, fluent and clearly adept at manipulating people. I am not impressed.'

The *Mirror* also noted the comments of parents who were less than impressed with the prison sentences dished out to other members of the Cambridge United crew who had been avenging an earlier sortie by Chelsea at a recent fixture. One parent was quoted as saying: 'It is political. Thatcher asked for tougher sentences and that is what the judge did.'

Furthermore, it was clear that the *Mirror* and judiciary had picked up on the way the young commander (Muranyi was 25) had 'led his gang with military style precision'.

Certainly the Casuals' concentration on forms of transport such as trains and coaches, recalling the rise of working-class leisure in the late nineteenth century when professional soccer was born, has given a new meaning to 'away-day'. West Ham's Inter-City Firm, Portsmouth's 6.57 Crew and others advertise that this is the age of the train in a way that Jimmy Saville never could. As Toby Young spotted for the *Observer*:

The media image of the football hooligan, of a skinhead 'bootboy' in Doctor Martens and drainpipe bleached denims, is hopelessly out of date. These days, there is a direct correlation between smartness of appearance and violent excess. The better dressed you are, the *harder* you are. The violent fans used to be the ones who arrived by train on the football specials laid on by British Rail; they belonged to the official supporters' clubs. Nowadays, all of the violence is concentrated in the unofficial supporter clubs, with their own names and their own newsletters.

Trains and vans and buses mean trouble
whether your team is playing or not (Chelsea
aggro found its way into Wembley for a non-
league final between Boston United and Weald-
stone in 1985) and once a team's reputation is
established it can pull in lads from miles away.

Police and press reaction to changes in the
forms of fan violence has been predictably slow
and ill-informed, cottoning on to its remnants
only when the styles have already moved on. In
the mass of print spilled over the Heysel
stadium disaster a team from the *Sunday Times*
observed, in contrast to Liverpool fans with 'rag-
ged jeans and do-it-yourself haircuts' that:

> Juventus' older supporters looked pred-
> ominantly *respectable*. Many stayed in de-
> cent hotels and planned to round off the
> trip with a good dinner. Though there is
> undoubtedly a smattering of Italian hooli-
> gans, most of the younger fans were con-
> spicuous by their bright designer clothes
> from Lacoste, Fiorucci and Benetton.

You bet they were conspicuous! To suggest that
looking respectable *means* respectability and
non-violent affluence in the 1980s is to be off
target by several football pitches. The new obsession with style is everywhere etched with
potential or actual violence and, whatever
might be more palatable, much of it is as proletarian as ever. The dole queue plus casual labour plus nicking equals Casual just as much as
displaced suburban yuppie imitators. And before the European Cup Final it was Italian
styles that were all the rage.

The mass media have always had their problems with 'football hooliganism', a label they
helped to create in the 1960s when the skin-
heads started to take ends, and after Liverpool
fans started the fashion of smashing trains like
Dr Beeching had never existed. Similarly, var-

Juventus keep up their end, Heysel 1985

ious political interests have misleadingly sought to claim hooligans *either* as the natural expression of the passion for real football (a man's game like it used to be; tough, rough and nasty) *or* as the pathological chauvinism of a minority of organized young fascists. The dimension in the 1980s which is there for all to wonder at and familiar to so many in post-Falklands Britain *combines* aspects of soccer hooliganism in a celebration of paranoid pride and masculine aggression. Furthermore, these are deregulated market forces on the frontline. As Martyn Harris wrote in *New Society* the year the task force set sail:

> A measure of crowd violence is endemic to football, precisely because football is an intensely competitive industry designed to create and harness strong emotions, especially in the young and bored. The leagues, divisions, promotions, relegations, cup ties and derbys are each attended by growing cash incentives, by savage, clinical professionalism on the field, and by the deliberate cultivation of tribal loyalties.

At home and abroad that competitiveness, mixed with, in Bobby Robson's phrase, the Falklands spirit and occasionally some booze, means that 'the lads', employed or not, dressed in designer clothes or stripped to the waist, are ready to prove their British manhood.

But where does this behaviour find its means of support? Football itself is one immediate realm. Alf Ramsey's designation of the Argenti-

nians as 'animals' after the infamous sending off
of Rattin in the World Cup match at Wembley in
1966 is often remembered but all England team
managers from Ramsey to Robson (with the possible exception of Joe Mercer) have planted the
seeds of nationalistic fervour with some well-
chosen words. One way of underscoring this has
been to constantly downgrade the talents of flair
players (Mercer tended to approve of flair, freedom and fun, even enjoyment), somehow imply-
ing that they are not quite the bulldog breed –
full of running, hard work and fish and chips.
The likes of Hoddle, Francis and all black
players remain on trial even late into their
careers.

There is clearly a sense in which the 1980s
lads, and many players and managers and
administrators in the modern game, are
Thatcher's boys much as we have come to see
prostitutes flocking down South from North of
Watford as 'Thatcher's Girls'. In the depths of
recession, selling sex as a commodity in the mar-
ketplace is a predictable aspect of a 'survival culture'. Similarly the worst hit areas of Britain,
geographically and industrially, have witnessed
a backlash of wounded masculine certainties. A
tough, traditional brand of masculinity, proved
by combat, is potentially on show every time a
League club or English national team takes the
field. Thatcher was wrong to link the Bradford
City fire with football violence but she was right
to see it as a metaphor for society – the one she
has contributed so much to since 1979. ■

5

Heysel, Heysel '85

" 'Course we're not the fuzz — we're plain-clothes hooligans!"

Loyalty and tradition, both local and national, are hardly in short supply in Thatcher's Britain. A fierce regionalism and pervasive populist nationalism mark out the 1980s, and football is an extraordinary barometer of such identities. Never before in the postwar era has there been such a sense of a divided nation: where the North and Midlands of England compare themselves so favourably to each other; where *within* such regions hatred and mutual jealousy run so deep; where the South East is despised by the other regions with such vitriolic envy. Not to mention the 'other' nations themselves – Scotland, Northern Ireland and Wales. Fans, players, managers and directors all participate in the national mass community pageant that is professional soccer in the 1980s against this knife-edge backdrop. 'Hooligans' mix it with 'foreigners' wherever they can be found, whether they're natives of Halifax or Buenos Aires; managers gleefully 'rejoice' in their 'lads' battles' and everybody worries whether black players really have got enough 'bottle'. Moreover, England's national side, especially on World Cup duty, contribute to a fresh conception of England without the Empire and the remaking of the working class in the image of a colonial adventure – uncannily like the counter-invasion of the Falklands/Malvinas in 1982. Jibes like 'Argentina, Argentina, what is it like to lose a war?' filled the air in Mexico in 1986 even as Argentina were convincingly settling a few old scores on the pitch, courtesy of Diego Maradona.

But in another sense such traditions and loyalties are redundant in Thatcher's Britain. Workers' loyalties to their enterprises are severely tested, though not necessarily broken, by mass bankruptcies and redundancies just as footballers' old tradition about one-club men being revered is now looking decidedly sour. Loyal 'servants' are being thrown on the

Loyal supporters

scrapheap as quick – if not quicker – than fly-by-night 'free agents'. Supporters' longstanding patience, too, is being subjected to whirlwind destruction as they cling to the wreckage of fond memory and special places on the bulldozed terraces. That 'spot' on the ground where so many have gathered for so many years will soon be finally cleared to be replaced by a supermarket check-out desk. They'll have paved paradise (the Kop end?) and put up a parking lot quicker than Burnley fell from the top to the bottom.

As Liverpool (and other English) fans showed at the European Cup Final at the Heysel stadium in May 1985, regional and national rivalries combined can gain European and World recognition (especially if given 'live' coverage on television) far more easily than the team, for all its glory, ever could. The 'scousers' managed to eclipse all previous attempts by British soccer followers to stamp their authority on Europe once and for all. Leeds United, Man. United, Celtic, Spurs and Rangers had all 'had a go' but it was only Liverpool who had a realistic chance of achieving the coveted goal. Their unrivalled record of continuous involvement in European competition stretching back into the 1960s had allowed those beloved stereotypical Merseysiders to thieve and fight their way across Europe bringing back the spoils of their conquests – scarves, jewellery or just the memories of bitter battles and unforgettable 'away' victories in the second leg. The team had also done its part on the pitch – adopting a 'European' style of play rather than a more traditional 'British' mode, slower and more defensive – bringing back home trophy after

Charge of the heavy brigade, Chelsea v. Sunderland 1985

trophy. The experience of previous seasons' hard campaigns stood team and supporters in good stead: cumulative experience on how to look after yourself on the continent and how to simultaneously assert the 'pride of Merseyside'.

As a consequence Heysel '85 was easy: dodg fences, unsatisfactory segregation and a wholl incompetent police force. No one consciousl meant for 39 to die but it was a timely warnin to rivals at home and abroad. 'Heysel, Heyse

'85', is as significant as 'Munich, Munich '58' in terrace culture, just like:

He's only a poor little wop
His face all tattered and torn

He made me feel sick so I hit him with a brick
And now he don't sing anymore.

Liverpool had certainly outclassed the rest: the

'lads had done well' in football jargon. All of this, predictably, was simply forgotten in the media coverage of the 'friendly' FA Cup Final between Liverpool and Everton in 1986. Nobody even mentioned the disruption of the community singing with 'You'll Never Walk Alone'!

Casual supporters

One thing that should have occurred to anyone watching the Heysel incident, in the flesh or 'live' on television, or for that matter the well-publicized events at football grounds in England over recent seasons – Luton v Millwall, Chelsea v Sunderland (and the return around Roker Park), Birmingham v Leeds, Liverpool v Man. United – was the demise of the 'typical' football hooligan of yesteryear (or since the 1960s anyway): the skinhead. At Heysel, St Andrews and elsewhere the public were treated to full frontal exposure of the new hooligan, quite different from the old, looking, as the *Mirror* put it, 'more like the boy next door than soccer hooligans'.

Not that there are no football fans who approximate to the traditional hooligan stereotype of the tabloid newspapers, but the emergence (and transformation every few weeks) of the Casuals on soccer terraces and stands has added a whole new look to football fashions. The development of the 'scallies' (Liverpool), Perries (Manchester) – originally (Fred) Perry Boys, now just 'boys' or 'lads' – and other regional variations since the late 1970s has coincided with the crisis of modern football. In that sense they represent a postmodern interlude in a sport which has rarely been fashion-conscious, though that other Merseyside team – Everton – started the 1985-6 season at Wembley in a televised Charity Shield game against Man. United looking (hair, kit, style) as sharp as some of their scouse followers. By the time the Casuals star-

ted getting nationwide publicity, the scene was set for panic measures such as the banning of away supporters in Europe and massive security back home. Press comment about 'casual' supporters being deterred by the introduction of a whole panoply of anti-hooligan devices ('hoolivans', electric fences, video cameras) never seemed to twig that the Casual supporters were in fact the most 'loyal'. Fans have long claimed allegiance to their clubs with the chant 'loyal supporters'; an answer, perhaps, to all the managers and secretaries' comments in club programmes which denounce the very same people for not being 'real' fans. As Hunter Davies found whilst people spotting for the colour supplement audience in his year at Spurs for the book *The Glory Game*, in an era when the 'skinhead' stereotype and football violence *were* more or less synonymous the resentment runs deep. One Spurs fan told him:

> The club call us hooligans, but who'd cheer them on if we didn't come? You have to stand there and take it when Spurs are losing and people are jeering at you. Its not easy. We support them everywhere, but we get no thanks.

Things don't change much in the football world. By the mid-1980s a different generation of football fans were still getting the same old song. Jimmy Frizzel, Assistant Manager of Man. City, told *Manchester Evening News*-reading fans in May 1985: 'We don't want you. You're not real fans, just a shameful minority who are doing nothing but wrecking the club's good name.'

Paul Hince, writing in the same paper from the perspective of a former player at Maine Road, weighed in behind the bosses:

> Let those morons be clear about one thing. The genuine decent City fans – and they

Keep off the grass! Arsenal v. Aston Villa 1981

are the *vast* majority – will be bitterly ashamed that the idiots who turned Meadow Lane into a battle zone should choose to wear the same sky blue favours.

Anyone who saw thousands of Man. City fans 'take' Oldham's Boundary Park on Easter Monday 1984 would have confidently predicted the events of May 1985 when Notts County went 3-0 up against a team who were expected to clinch promotion later that day. (Billy McNeill's Blue and White Army had been singing 'We'll be up, We'll be up, We'll be up at 5 o'clock' all day in and around Nottingham pubs.) City fans' pitch 'invasion' was nothing compared to the stylish and relatively peaceful swamping of Oldham a year earlier but massive publicity drew the stock replies. As club chairman, Peter Swales, put it:

> We are paying the price for having one of the country's biggest away followings because hooligans are latching on. The people causing the aggro are certainly not the ones I meet when visiting branches of our supporters club.

City's 'Junior Blues' support is massively undercut by the 'Maine Line Crew' who travel on Mayne's luxury coaches to away matches (first stop Piccadilly Station approach) and serve as the hard core of the club's 'loyal' supporters. These fans *are* Man. City. If the team isn't doing the business on the park (and City fans' chants in the two seasons they were in the Second division included 'Will We Ever Win Again?', 'We're So Shit It's Unbelievable') the 'other', reserve side waiting on the terraces or the expensive seats will do it in the opponents' 'end', pubs, shopping centre, railway or tube station. When managers talk about 'battling' teams *two* of his club's sides are out there: it's no coincidence that fans describe themselves as 'armies'.

In the 1980s, the spectre of the skins stomping across football's peaceful past – when Pompey Chimes didn't include the response 'Fuck Off, Pompey' and West Ham fans conducted the community singing of 'I'm Forever Blowing Bubbles', or so the old story goes – since the 1967-8 football season, with the odd 'glam' interval in between, has all but faded. Bands of 'rough' fans still 'all follow Man. United', or whoever, but the Casuals' ever changing mood (and clothing, hair and so on) has gone hand in hand with the post-punk emergence of 'fighting crews' complete with embossed calling cards and plenty of television gab when the documentary programme makers come a-calling. Most fans' response to *Hooligan*, an ITV 'show' transmitted in August 1985 which featured West Ham's famed ICF or 'Inter-City Firm' was explicit – 'ICF, wank, wank, wank'! The Casual style has emphasized respectability and apparently mainstream look, *not* marking out the majority of fans as hooligans for the police, observers and stewards. An undifferentiated mass – unless you know what to look for, and even then it will have changed around again – just as in the 1930s photographs of crowd scenes at football grounds, apparently containing the odd rascal but no real troublemakers, if the nostalgic photo-histories are to be believed. Trad and modern styles however are being mixed up and mocked in the same way the team styles in 1980s football are trying to ape 'Continental' and 'English' formats without resolving the way the two cultures clash. Past and present concocted together in a bizarre mish-mash. What else can we make of Merseyside scallies, wearing Pink Floyd and Bob Dylan T-shirts, stoned out of their brains on the Anfield Kop? Born-again hippies, a psychedelic revival pure and simple? Or another crazy twist in the regional post-modern condition of soccer which has flourished since the demise of punk? If that was an unpredictable reaction, like punk never existed, the effect was to confuse an already fast-changing, fashion-conscious football scene.

Relationships of identity between teams and their support is based on this aspect of ways to be winning. The style of Liverpool's success in the 1984-5 season was dull, predictable, on the defensive after the transfer of Souness to the Italian job. Compared to Everton's exciting (for the 1980s – perhaps only Aston Villa in their Championship winning season have matched it)

style in their surge to the Canon League title and victory in the European Cup Winners Cup Final in May 1985, it was like the contrast between the respective supporters at the two European finals. Contrast the publicity given to

" *This kid's years ahead of his time – a protest footballer!* "

West Ham's Trevor Brooking, 1984

Everton's 'peaceful' fraternizing with Dutch police and the violent confrontations of Liverpool and Juventus fans and the Belgian riot police. West Ham's ICF puts paid to the Hammers' long standing reputation for a lack of 'steel' better than all Billy Bonds's tackles in the 1970s put together. The midfield 'softness' at football's 'Academy' was always well known. Brian Clough's cryptic description of Trevor Brooking as a player who floats like a butterfly and stings like one (Nottingham Forest players always reckoned clever Trevor didn't like to get his shorts dirty) was one of his more memorable lines though it didn't stop Brooking commenting in his autobiography that:

> the terraces . . . are no longer safe places and this will not change until discipline returns to our society . . . These young people would experience a severe shock if they had to submit to the discipline of professional football.

Tough but tender, or what? Man. United's reintroduction of wingers like Jesper Olsen and Peter Barnes, gave them their best stylistic fight-back for years (Steve Coppell and Gordon Hill in the Tommy Docherty era were always more midfield harriers going forward than 'genuine' traditional wingers). It helped to bury, in the public mind at least, the memory of the Stretford End baying 'We hate humans' in response to being branded as animals by media people everywhere. United in the 1970s 'took' more clubs than former Preston North End hard man Tommy 'Doc' had in his bag (Docherty's favourite line has always been 'more clubs than Jack Nicklaus') and it was only with the boredom of the Dave Sexton era (all pop, *no* style), when a length of the field run by centre-half Gordon McQueen could bring the house down, that the Red Army fiction died a death.

What counts in the 1980s book is the assertion of *new* identities, based on regional peculiarities, differences and rivalries to overlay the older, traditional hatreds. Whether in fanzines like Merseyside's *The End* or style house journals like *The Face* the new spirit of football watching (and playing) is evidently abroad. In the 1984-5 football season we were told:

> Now the football season is underway, there's a great difference in style between North and South. The Cockneys are still trying to buy the most expensive clothes available, while the North is wearing 21″ flares with an untucked Ben Sherman shirt.
>
> Knowing the Cockneys they'll now be scouring Bond Street for Gucci flares.

This flash of a Sheffield blade runner stirred the passions of *Face* readers like a bloody Stanley knife brandished over the electric fence at Stamford Bridge ('We love Stanley, he's our friend' and they don't mean Stanley Matthews!). Judging by the volume of correspondence 1985 was indeed a year of changing football fashions. Not that one letter to *The Face* was enough to convince everybody though. 'Someone who enjoys fashion' retorted to a southern (Spurs) fan from Norwich:

> Reading the letter about Norwich's casual scene who is 'Casual' trying to kid? Not Norwich people, that's for sure. Maybe he's just trying to influence other casuals to dress in the same stuff for another couple of years.
>
> 'Interesting to note the re-emergence of Adidas and Nike' is it? What a load of bollocks! What's interesting about training shoes, Aquascutum and Liberty? *Whoopee*! As far as trend and fashion is

concerned, does he not think it's *all* 'well played out'?

> If Norwich is classed as a dressing backwater, he has only himself, and others who dress like him, to blame. And if Lacoste is still here for another summer, I'm moving.

Never mind the bollocks (and much of it certainly is, as all the arguments in *The End* and other fanzines testify) of the latest on football's scene. Casual style is constantly changing – dressing up, dressing down, and dressing up again – in the quest for exclusivity, even if its only for a day or so that, as David Bowie (the most important influence on the styles of the 1970s and 1980s that became Casual style) put it, 'we can all be heroes'. All dressed up and nowhere to go but the Job Centre or the football, Britain's male youth in the 1980s – working or not – have played havoc with standard conceptions of what professional football means. The fads themselves mean less than Prince's foray into Paisley and psychedelia: what's hard to shake off is the impression that in the year *after* Nineteen Eighty Four *all* that's left is the next day's model and local pride. Their Manc rivals continue to taunt the Merseyside teams – success stories in a city bankrupted by Thatcherism – with the chant:

> In your Liverpool slums
> You look in the dustbin for something to eat
> You find a dead rat and think it's a treat
> In your Liverpool slums.

Variations on a traditional theme, just like the teams' differing playing styles. But for good measure a dash of Thatcherite 'realism' for the less well-off regions as voiced in:

One job between you
You've only got one job between you.

Who needs the Department of the Environment when you've got neighbours like these? And in any case what *has* become of masculine certainty and traditional values when what you wear to the match depends on the design (no longer the colours) and origin of your scarf?

A tale of two nations

After the Heysel disaster a Sunday newspaper ran a story on a tale of two cities: Turin, where Juventus are based, and Liverpool. It concentrated on the relative affluence of the Italian city, even in a country which is traditionally seen as one of the sick men of Europe, and the nearly absolute poverty (moral and economic) of the

Italian fighting crew at Heysel

city of Merseybeat and Bill Shankly. It bemoaned the fact that, as Shankly had told everyone years before, on Merseyside soccer seemed to be a modern religion and concluded that Juventus's 1-0 European Cup Final victory symbolized more than the difference between two of the best footballing club sides in the world: it was a sign of how degenerate the once great seaport had become. Italian style beats Liverpool style hands down, anyday, was the clear message. Journalist Edward Vulliamy followed similar themes, in the immediate after-

Juventus fans strike back

math of Brussels, when he argued in the *New Statesman* that somehow Italy's opiate of the masses was more sacred than our own:

> Football in Italy is a religion – not without violent devotees, but violence is swamped by the fanatical interest among all social classes. Last year, when Liverpool went to Rome to win the European Cup by beating their hosts, the AC Roma supporters sang in the stadium for five hours before kick off. After defeat, fires lit up all around the ground in the balmy dusk. A riot? No, it was the fans burning every flag, scarf, banner and hat they had, in complete silence: an extraordinary ritual. In the streets outside, true, some threw bottles at the English. But many more – grown men – wept on their knees in gutters. The city plunged into deep and heartfelt despair and shame for weeks. And when Juventus won the Italian league a few weeks before, celebrations in the streets of Turin and other cities lasted three nights. Almost nobody turned up for work at Turin's Fiat factory the day after the winning match.

This rose-coloured pic of Italian football watching is almost as one-dimensional as the never-ending media build-up about foreigners' (especially Italians') footballing brutality. Even the ones who don't kick you or spit on you or grab your balls (really close marking) in a clinch, take bribes, don't they? Fleet Street's comic-strip racism is simply inverted in these accounts of the essential 'niceness' of Italian style. In fact the Italian fans' treatment of Liverpool supporters in the 1984 European Cup Final *was* another factor in the melting pot of Heysel a year later and was yet another memory of a tough continental fixture.

The connections between the nations of England and Italy and their major cities and football teams are much more complex than this rehabilitation of the Latin temperament syndrome allows. Italian football hooliganism has modelled itself on the publicity given to English, and other British, fans over the past twenty years and on direct experience of the phenomenon through confrontation at European, international or simply friendly matches. Italian style has been influential not only in the fashion industry in the same period but has periodically gained dominance on the football field. The Italian national team's victory in the 1982 World Cup Final in Spain against the 'might' of the West Germans managed to atone for many past misdeeds as well as renewing a growing belief – through Conti – in stylish wing play. Battles with Arsenal at Highbury were temporarily shoved aside, gone but certainly not forgotten. And of course the Italians *looked* good.

What is also missed in the one-sided rush to overemphasize Italian football virtues (though there *are* more female football followers in Italy, a country where prospective English female professional footballers have to go to ply their trade, banned in their home nation) is the significance of the Casuals' development in places like Manchester and Merseyside at a time when those cities are de-industrializing at a faster rate and with more horrific social consequences than even their Italian counterparts. Their expensive style is a stinging reminder of what the supposedly affluent 1980s count for and how international the style wars have become. There were some 'traditional' football hooligans at Heysel (stripped down, drunk as hell) but what

the fighting Juventus fans were wearing wasn't lost on the fashion conscious English boys; starting pistols and flag poles pale into insignificance when it comes to sharp shoes and haircuts. This is the same snap shot of 'enterprise culture' which sees thousands of 'scrapheap' citizens, old and young, in 1980s Britain living stylishly off the local council rubbish tip. If you can't beat 'em, look as if you can.

The starkest illustration of Britain as a divided nation is in the relationship between the ever more exclusive style of the 'elite' of the First division (and the Premier League in Scotland) and the rest. It's not just the lower reaches of the Third and Fourth divisions that house football's poor relations. And with the lessening of the differences between non-League and Football League grounds, playing styles, levels of skill and fitness, the so-called best League competition in the World (now the Italians must find that *really* funny) is symbolized by a mere half a dozen clubs and a few 'star' players. Life below the breadline is increasingly based on an 'informal economy' which sees: rich clubs buying seventeen year old 'prospects' and immediately loaning them back to the nearly bankrupt selling club so that they can survive at least another season; club fittings ('carpet for the manager's office, sir?') bought from someone who'd just fallen off the back of a lorry; meals *en route* to away games curtailed in favour of a Mars bar each (helps you work, rest and *play*) or equivalent travellers' fare. Jack Butterfield, general manager of Merseyside's third team, Tranmere Rovers, in 1982 spoke of the hard work that goes into losing *only* £100,000 a year:

> At Tranmere our average gate receipts are £1,800. From that about £600 goes to the visitors, £500 to the police and in VAT, and £170 in direct match expenses. Only £500 is left towards meeting a weekly wage bill

of £3,100. And that is without any appearance money and bonuses which we are committed to pay. After paying rates, lighting, and telephones and slicing down to the bone, the most optimistic forecast for a year is a loss of £100,000.

Later League rulings on home clubs keeping gate money (except of course in the moneyspinning – FA Cup ties against 'top' opposition) didn't really help save the Tranmeres of the football world – fairy godfathers from across the seas were more influential in last-minute rescue from oblivion – but it is easy to see why Sheffield United entered into its long-running battle over the responsibility for policing costs of their home matches at Bramall Lane.

Manchester's nearest poverty stricken neighbour, Stockport County, is typical of Fourth (and many Third and Second) division clubs struggling to make a loss in the shadow (which can mean anything up to fifty miles) of more illustrious 'big city' outfits. Bright lights are out, even down in some cases. In 1986 'proud' Preston's floodlight pylons lay crestfallen *outside* their Deepdale ground, like some giant central defenders felled by a late tackle.

For County, too, much of the club's money is going on paying debts and repaying loans to directors who talk not about football but how their lottery is doing and where the players' wages are coming from. One Stockport director when asked whether the club's financial dilemma might affect their play replied: 'Not really, as long as they get their wages. The only thing that really affects them in this situation is if one of them is injured because they know they have to carry him.'

The 'gap' between actual and necessary playing squads in the majority of clubs in the English League has been met in many instances by the exploitation of the country's newest youth policy, the Youth Training Scheme. In this new monetarist version of 'jobs for the boys' (in contrast to the 'elite' soccer school at Lilleshall intended to put flair back into the system addicts of the playground) history repeats itself. As the *Sunday Times* noted in the 1983-4 season:

Has English professional football come full circle in the century? In the 1880s when professionalism first crept into the game clubs used to advertise for players and offer them jobs in the local factories to supplement their income. Today the same thing is happening, albeit discreetly, in the lower regions of the Football League.

Crippled by falling gates and mounting debts clubs have emulated the tactics of Victorian millowners in finding devious ways of slashing their wage bill. Their principal obstacle was their contractual obligations to players they sign. This guarantees the player a minimum wage, pension rights, accident insurance and redundancy. They have circumvented this by employing players eager to make the grade without a contract at all, just a loose verbal agreement, or taking on youngsters on the Youth Training Scheme, or both. This season there are nearly 200 players without contracts and some 500 YTS players, totalling more than a quarter of all League players.

Non-contract players take the field at their own risk and for a pittance. Some earn as little as £20 a week, are not covered if they are seriously injured, and can be slung out of the game at a moment's notice without any compensation. The lucky ones spend their afternoons working in the firm of a benevolent director.

In many respects, for many clubs, the 'new' youth policy is simply a continuation of age-old practices which didn't die with the turn of the century but carried on right into the heart of the modern age of soccer. However, they have certainly undercut the 'natural' channels from school to club (apprenticeship and 'schoolboy') which have been decimated by recession-hit League clubs.

As Mickey Burns of the PFA pointed out in May 1985, 'From our point of view the Youth Training Scheme has been a godsend because many soccer youth schemes had disappeared'. Very few YTS players make the 'grade' (even fewer than under the old merciless system) but Burns claimed:

> many of those who won't make it as professional players have been kept on in other roles – in the office, on the ground staff, and at least one as a trainee physiotherapist. Under YTS the youngsters are learning more than just soccer skills. Some clubs would prefer trainees to concentrate on soccer but through the YTS the youngsters are learning other skills which will help them to earn a living in leisure and recreation, wheather they fail to make it as players or go on to play for 15 years. If I was starting now in soccer I would ask to go on a YTS course rather than apprenticeship, because I would be better prepared for a career if I did or didn't make it in football. Last year clubs had to take three apprentices for every two trainees, but this year most clubs have taken only trainees.

Yet it's not only young players who are suffering at the hands of football's cutbacks. Young *and* 'old' crocks are still subject to the ruthlessness of club management – always there but now most definitely in the ascendancy – prepared to push teams onto the park however many of them are partially or wholly unfit. Fitness tests increasingly add up to 'you're fit this week or you won't play for us again' as harassed bosses, particularly in the lower divisions, perm an eleven from thirteen or fourteen men squads. Injuries which never quite heal simply lead to a collection on the insurance for the club (at least one big club now deems it too expensive to insure its players; they'd rather pay out transfer fees instead of high premiums) and a quick trip to the dole office for the 'obedient' servant, the player. One Second division player who cost his club £80,000 in transfer fee in the 1980s found himself selling KP nuts a few months later after sustaining a serious injury, a salutory lesson for budding Charlie Nicholases seduced by the roar of the (ever declining) madding crowd and the sweet smell of the linament oil. Football's long standing paternalism is finally caving in to allow 'market forces' to push out quicker than ever those who can't survive with the fittest. Darwin not Darwen is the name football now recalls from nineteenth-century history.

With fifty per cent of the attendances in the Second and Third division lost over the last decade it is remarkable that a large minority of League clubs have not gone the way of either Accrington Stanley or Workington Town. What's certain is that the most likely contenders are from Britain's older industrial regions with strong footballing traditions (South Wales, the North West, the North East) and the predictable replacements, representatives of the new high-tech nirvana, from Middlesbrough to Maidenhead.

Who'll support you evermore?

Football is one of the few aspects of popular culture which has almost entirely resisted 'Americanization'. Tough, traditional masculinity is what modern football has come to mean as opposed to 'Rambo'-like (apologies to Norman Whiteside not intended) American pro-football, now set to catch on in Britain thanks to Channel 4 exposure. In the wake of football's decline, snooker's popularity might be taking the eye but American sports – like basketball as well as pro-football – are fast catching up on the outside.

Nice, 'clean' pursuits, ripe for trouble-free sponsorship as football goes down the plughole. A British audience, especially amongst the young, is assured and things look bright for the 1990s whereas football is struggling to convince a doubting public that after Bradford and Heysel it really will be all right on Wednesday night or Saturday afternoon.

The notion that attendances of a few thousand people at a lowly League game is insufficient *per se* and justifies wholesale closure of the temples of doom is a logic foisted on the nation by the insatiable demands of sponsorship and the media. As Hugh McIlvanney mused about the false prophets of football's demise in 1982, lamentations about gates of 1,500 at soccer 'outposts' such as Darlington are misplaced:

> what other sport performed at so humble a level could expect to draw more in such an area; they couldn't get two and a half thousand to turn out and watch the town hall burn down.

That there has been decline in attendances at professional soccer matches is unarguable. Since the Second World War there has been a rise to a peak of 41 million in the 1948-9 season

One down, 17 million to go

but a steady decrease ever since, to 33 million a year in the 1950s to 27 million in the 1960s, plummeting in the season of the Heysel and Bradford disasters to just under 18 million. A MORI poll for the *Sunday Times* in the aftermath of Brussels concluded that the remaining soccer fans prepared to click through the turnstiles every other week are:

> still overwhelmingly male. They are also predominantly young; among the middle-aged and pensioners only 3 per cent go to matches three or more times a year, compared to 14 per cent in the 15-24 age group.

How small soccer's audience really is in the 1980s, compared to the salad days of the immediate post-war boom period has only recently dawned on television companies, now much more prepared to go for the League jugular. Viewing figures for recorded soccer highlights have dropped by over half in less than a decade and it is ever more clear that only the 'big match' between 'top' teams, such as the European Cup Final at Heysel or England's patchy performances in the Mexico World Cup, can guarantee a massive television audience. Only FA Cup ties and major European competition (before the post-Heysel ban) sustain a mass interest on the terraces, too, unless the team is challenging for promotion or championship or involved in 'lovable' local derbies. Yet football is still statistically and emotionally the national game; three times as many people watch it as watch any other sport live. As the *Sunday Times* noted, reporting public opinion poll data in the wake of the 56 deaths at Bradford and 39 at Heysel, the threat of violence, the advantages of watching soccer on telly instead of at the ground, the expense and the lack of entertainment were the most obvious reasons cited by football fan respondents for their continued absence from the game's 'authentic' pleasures. The background was clear:

> Apart from the effects of football violence, changes like increased car-ownership, a shorter working week and new leisure patterns are seen as the most significant factors in [football's] decline. By 1980 football had dropped behind swimming, darts, golf and snooker in the nation's top 10 participation sports and 100,000 joggers had taken to the streets and parks.
>
> Throughout this [post-war] period soccer failed to respond to an increasingly competitive market for people's leisure time. Admission prices at matches soared, pushed upwards in part by the abolition of the maximum wage for players and ever more exotic transfer fees, culminating in the £1.5 million paid by Manchester United for Bryan Robson in 1981 . . . Massed and monied ranks of sponsors, advertisers and the media . . . seem to back Mrs Thatcher's mood for change. Soccer is definitely not the big sell of the 1960s and 1970s.

Heysel's violent images relayed round the world (even *Time* magazine thought Britain newsworthy that week) played havoc with general public perceptions but football followers — though the overwhelming majority were repulsed — knew it could have happened sooner or later at British grounds anywhere during the modern age. They were less likely to be put off the next home game by the immediate impact of

Heysel than by the stepping up of surveillance by closed-curcuit television and general militarization of football grounds which had already been taking place for twenty years or more.

The reason for football's lingering so long in the memory is its continuing connection with growing up masculine in Britain today. Heysel was a complex sign of local and national male identity just as much as trudging down to Gresty Road on a Friday night to catch Crewe against Torquay. There's as much trouble at Third and Fourth division grounds in the higher echelons and when it does break out the same pleasures emerge. As Arthur Hopcraft (who else?) noted in the book of the game:

> The point about football in Britain is that it is not just a sport people take to, like cricket or tennis or running long distances. It is inherent in the people. It is built into the urban psyche, as much a common experience to our children as our uncles and school . . . It has more significance in the national character than theatre has . . . It has not been only a game for 80 years: not since the working classes saw it as an escape route out of drudgery and claimed it as their own. It has not been a sideshow this century. What happens on the football field matters, not the way that food matters but as poetry does to some people and alcohol does to others: it engages the personality.

That such male obsession could outlive the Heysel and Bradford events – and indeed even gain sustenance from them in terms of both reputation for 'hardness' and bravado – should not be surprising. After all if the year of 1985 meant Heysel *and* Madonna, Bruce Springsteen – a veritable musical Sly Stallone, all brother's pride – was not very far behind in the stakes of popularity. His traditionalism and patriotism might have been misunderstood by America's B-movie actor at the helm (Springsteen gave generously to British miners' support groups as he had done to blue-collar causes in his own hometown) but he gave a post-Vietnam performance to rival *The Deerhunter*'s finale. His songs of dented national and local faith (always through male eyes) sound like a US version of so many terrace chants. They resemble the disillusionment of run of the mill, loyal club 'servants' who see their brethren packing their kit-bags for the continental stage only to be struck down by injury or club closure themselves. Heysel's potential to be Britain's Vietnam is not really so fanciful; national disgrace followed by national penitence followed by national rehabilitation: a process that is already well in hand. ∎

Over the top, Chelsea v. Liverpool 1982

6

You're not singing anymore

" This is what I CALL football violence!"

It was entirely predictable that football followers would be 1985's 'enemy within' for the Thatcher government. What better 'alien' force for the Iron Lady (crocodile tears and all) to take on after vanquishing the 'argies' and the miners? Soccer 'louts' would be an easy and popular prize for a 'law-and-order' party; the completion of an historic treble, you might say, in as many years. Set up a 'war' cabinet, encourage the further development of a National Reporting Centre-style policing operation headed by a tough, uncompromising police chief like James Anderton, and reap an electoral harvest. This may have been the original battle plan but the war is already proving to be something else altogether. And the casualties, in the long term, will include civil liberties – such as they presently exist – and professional football in Britain as we have known it for the last twenty years.

Part of the difficulty facing Mrs Thatcher after televized highlights of the battles of Kenilworth Road (Luton v Millwall) flickered onto her screen was that though her second task force was soon to be despatched – hurried along by events at Bradford, Birmingham and Brussels – the fans themselves were often celebrating precisely the combination of Victorian and modern values which made up the Falklands style in 1982 and which – back home – did so much to break the mining communities in 1984-5. Task force style looked pretty close to what the 'new' enemy within were cooking up for most of the late 1970s and the 1980s. More than this, it is possible to see in the language of battles, armies and other military metaphors – never far away in football culture – a national obsession with hard working, 'professional' attitudes to the exclusion of football's 'magic' – the skilful, stylish player who can turn a game in a split second but do nothing for the rest of the ninety minutes. Media 'experts' spotlight action like John Barnes' 'Brazilian' type goal in the Maracana

stadium (which in the event only helped him back on to the subs bench) merely to question such players' commitment.

Then the same 'experts' complain when the tarnished players reach for their passports and Swiss bank accounts and sell their wares in Leagues which appreciate their style. An anti-Europeanism parades itself alongside a more general sense of xenophobia in English soccer culture which takes great sustenance from much of the Thatcher government style. How ironic that the fashion modes of the Casual supporters who are on the receiving end of government initiatives were 'pinched' (in many cases literally) on trips to their teams' games throughout Europe over the past decade. And in 1985-6 that the clubs themselves were banned from European competition in the wake of the Heysel disaster.

An inability of radical opponents of Thatcher's government policies to move beyond conceptions of football hooliganism which were only relevant – if then – in an era when modern football was dying, has left the field open for the Tories. But identity cards, bans on alcohol, increased surveillance through closed circuit television and video will only succeed in further displacing trouble from the terraces to the stands and into the streets, shopping centres, pubs and railway stations. This process has been detectable for years now and police arrest figures inside grounds (said to be rapidly decreasing with the introduction of all the new measures) are ever more misleading. Many of the First division, and some Second division, grounds have long been so strictly monitored and segregated that they are like top security prisons, with few escapees. And it was Labour's Dennis Howell – former referee and now wheeled into television studios as the man in the middle of raving Tories and loony lefties in football debates – who was responsible for the introduction of 'caging' in of fans in the modern era, so don't expect any liberal solutions there. If Thatcher and her cronies have their way there will probably be only a few clubs left before this century is out and the increasingly desperate battles of 'barmy armies' will be taking place elsewhere – Test match cricket perhaps?

The enemy within

The old stomping ground of soccer hooliganism as a political football is suddenly shifting. Once elevated to the personal target of the Prime Minister the professional game in England is being shaken to its foundations. Its administrators are to be seen scurrying back from far-off places just to meet with the occupant of No. 10 Downing Street, whose interest in the sport has so recently been captured. Both Labour and Tory governments in the modern era have expressed their concern with the problems of 'public disorder' around football matches and, moreover, their responses have proved to be remarkably similar. But the 1980s, if you believe press and television comment – and that is after all almost the entire source of information for the present set of government ministers – have witnessed a veritable explosion. Crews ambushing crews often means *less* likelihood of injury to bystanders but the law-and-order campaigns of the popular press in the 1980s have gone into overdrive on the 'menace' of football hooligans. Headlines like 'Weapons of Shame' preface increasingly familiar match reports in the tabloids in this decade:

An evil array of weapons was found yesterday as police swooped on two trains carrying bloodthirsty soccer fans.

The armoury included knuckle-dusters, staves, knives and a bottle of ammonia.

Officers found FORTY-TWO implements of hate hidden under seats and scattered along the track near Richmond station, South London.

They acted on a tip-off that 50 armed thugs were on their way to the Spurs-Chelsea match which ended in a 1-1 draw with 13 arrests.

The quantity of press reporting (that is, column inches) might not have changed that much in the last ten years but the precise form of football hooliganism has become a media obsession, even if it is constantly mistaken. 'Forest Fans Go On Knife Rampage' headlined a story about Nottingham Forest's trip to Bruges for the return leg of a UEFA Cup tie; 'Fans in Fire Bomb War' introduced an account of an Inter City Firm attack on Millwall fans travelling to an away game against Sheffield United; 'Slash Victim' denoted the increasingly familiar news story of a fan being slashed by a Stanley knife, in this case at a Blackpool away match at Torquay. When Chelsea's young reserve, Bobby Isaacs, was badly cut by Millwall fans as he turned up at a senior game to watch his team play at the Den, the papers screeched 'Soccer Super Boy Is Knifed' and 'Footballer Slashed By Mob'. The danger to players from the 'mob' was constant fodder for roving reporters keeping their eyes on the field, too. Clive Walker's infamous greeting at the hands of a Chelsea fan as he returned to Stamford Bridge with Sunderland drew widespread publicity, as did the dangers of goalkeeping. Ask Steve Hardwick of Oxford United, who claimed 'I was not hurt, but it terrified me' when Leeds United went down 5-2 on Maxwell's Manor, or Les Sealey of Luton who had never run faster than the night he fled Kenilworth Road's invading Millwall fans, if they still think (Wim Wenders, where are you now?) that the goalkeeper's only fear is of the penalty.

The old favourites of a bygone football hooligan age are still with us, of course. 'Savages', 'Uglies', 'Scum', 'Rowdies' jostle for position with 'Rampage', 'Riot', 'Battlefield', 'Ambush' on front, centre or back pages only to be repeated with visual captions on the same night's television news. 'Shame', 'Night of Madness', 'Bloody Disgrace', 'Bloody Face of Soccer' still greet us at the breakfast table like a video nasty shopping list. Occasionally the understatement slips through (though not very often) – 'I'm Afraid That Where There's Trouble You Will Always Find Our Keith' seemed somewhat inappropriate after the rioting at the France v England game in Paris when the *Sunday People* started to question the parents of jailed English fans. Even then it is only in the same vein as general news reporting which tells us that Britons are *not* involved when another airliner ploughs into the runway. The urge to discover the *causes* of such 'mindless madness' (why *do* the morons do what they do to you?) is undiminished, turning up adolescence ('Thugs Aged Thirteen In Riot Shock') alcohol ('Soccer in Shame as Drunken Louts Wreck New Cars') and even cannabis:

Lunatic England Soccer fans on their way to last night's International in Luxembourg beat a booze ban – by getting stoned on drugs.

They knew cross-Channel ferries and coaches would be 'dry', so the bovver-boys smoked vast amounts of cannabis instead. The result – when they arrived for the big match they were as 'high' as if they were drunk. And they soon found the trouble they were looking for. Police arrested 32 England fans BEFORE the kick off.

And after the match they went on an orgy of destruction. A hospital was under siege until nursing nuns pleaded with the fans to go away for the sake of the patients.

The wild-eyed mob then turned on parked cars, lifting them bodily. As police moved in the English youths raced down the street smashing every window.

More than 1,000 Luxembourg riot troops charged the mob and finally herded them into the railway station.

I travelled on a Luxembourg-bound coach from London's Waterloo station – and before we reached the suburbs, cannabis cigarettes were being rolled.

Joints were passed around the 50-seater bus during the 16-hour journey, and teenage boys were openly smoking the drug.

The air was heavy with the smell of cannabis.

It was so much easier for our intrepid investigators in the good old days when soccer hooligans wore boots and braces and students and hippies smoked 'funny cigarettes'. It's enough to give journalism a bad name and the reporters themselves a nervous breakdown. Typically such uncertainty crept in when a *News Of The World* team reporting on the aftermath of the notorious Birmingham City v West Ham United FA Cup tie (another in the long list of pitch invasions when only a 'fresh pair of legs' will get 'result' – West Ham were 3-0 down when the boys went over the top) focused on an alleged

member of the ICF, who spilled the beans:

> You wouldn't suspect him of being a thug. He doesn't wear the London side's claret and blue scarf. He never chants. He always wears expensive jackets, smart slacks and casual shoes. And talking of his hooligan gang – the dreaded Inter City Firm – he says 'We look like a bunch of Young Conservatives' . . . he told how he stands with other ICF thugs where they can cause the most trouble – right in the middle of the other team's fans. 'For away games', he said, 'we usually travel by train, that's where we get our nickname. But the police are getting too smart, so we've started getting coaches, too . . . We'll get there nice and early. Dressed as we are the Old Bill will probably direct us to a nice spot in the car park. We don't just want to smash up the other fans, we aim for total domination. We want to feel like kings in the football world and tread the other scum into the dirt. You only get into the firm by having bottle. You never run, even if its 100 to one . . . Some of the hardest lads look like students with woolly beards and glasses. They're the ones who'll pull a blade.'

No wonder the Fleet Street boozers are full: it must be very confusing! When the *Mirror* can imagine that Casuals have to be forced to wear their expensive gear *so that* the police will be outwitted, perhaps it's not so surprising that other rags have apoplexy when they discover post-punks on dope and football crews with woolly beards and glasses.

The boys next door

Worse than this for the media and politicians alike is the continual refusal of the 'enemy within' to stand still, even for a moment. Though tabloid papers' pen pictures of firms crews in the 1980s do occasionally get it right, they need to remember that the names the 'lads' give themselves often change over as quickly as the trains they catch on an awayday (often paid for by Persil tickets, just like everybody else). It all depends on which journalist or television reporter is doing the interview. And the nature and form of the crews are in almost permanent transition – exactly as Casual style itself is in a continual state of decay and recycle.

Here comes the judge

When the 1985 'Tottenham' riots hit the headlines (Broadwater Farm not White Hart Lane, though ironically Spurs' home games were cancelled in its wake) the 'law-and-order' card had been played so successfully in the field of football that government fortunes were riding considerably higher than could have been expected for a party ruling four million unemployed.

The Popplewell inquiry and new Public Order Act proposals on top of judges' terrace-like surge to impose long-term jail sentences on *any* football related misdemeanours added up to a formidable onslaught on football's disorderly house. Mr Justice Popplewell, appointed after Birmingham and Bradford, then asked to come on for extra-time following the Brussels debacle, did the Prime Minister's dirty work almost as well as her remaining toadying cabinet colleagues. Brian Glanville – a journalist known for not venturing out of the South East Thatcher-style, even though his Italian connections are impeccable – assessed the interim report of m'learned fan from the bench with (in typically 1950s, nostalgic tones) 'Two Cheers For Popplewell'. Glanville thought:

The Popplewell Report goes some of the way; but not quite far enough. In suggesting the banning of away fans at professional matches, it has produced the only rational, feasible answer to football's violence, the elimination of potential enemies. In proposing as a corollary, the issue of identity cards, it has fallen into the government's own error of seeing something quite impracticable as a panacea . . . Could away fans be banned without implementing identity cards? I don't see why not; except in the case of local derbies (which should always be played in the morning). It has been tried before . . . Mrs Thatcher is among those who believe fervently in identity cards . . . What hope would football have of retaining the great floating, uncommitted population of fans with no particular preference, those who make the difference between penury and profit to a club.

Popplewell's final report ('Football is Dead, Long Live Football') shifted ground from his earlier, rushed findings in the summer of '85 where he earned Thatcher's thanks for his call for identity card systems and total bans on travelling supporters. His conclusion was to recommend new laws intended to outlaw violence and racist chanting inside grounds where soccer, rugby and cricket are played. Let snooker players snort coke, but Popplewell doesn't like professional footballers because they generally 'cheat' and behave in a disorderly fashion which stirs up trouble amongst the fans. Executive boxes are reprieved from booze bans by the sober judge and for the rest of us much more heavy surveillance and control are recommended.

As Rob Hughes put it in the *Sunday Times* response, the measures are comparable to the installation of machine guns at British airport terminals and serve to further turn our sports grounds into sites which are more akin to concentration camps than pleasure palaces. As Hughes said:

> What Popplewell has observed on his rounds, and what those who attend football grounds, out of choice or occupation, have also come to recognize, is that much is being done inside and out to make our sporting Saturdays a police state day.

Popplewell's recommendations on the future safety of grounds may still be the last, final, deepest cut of all for up to half of all Football League clubs (it is unlikely that in the next few years many of them will be able to meet the post-Bradford conditions) but his 'new order' for football will give the police and courts their biggest licence yet. Thatcher's kingdom will be no place for *any* football fans in the late 1980s if the full implications of the public order changes are realized in the aftermath of football's watershed year of 1985. The offence of 'disorderly conduct' is designed to *formally* criminalize shouting, swearing and 'rowdy' behaviour or 'hooliganism'. Police powers are extended in the most sweeping way since 'sus', allowing the power of arrest over anybody whose language or behaviour is likely to cause harassment, alarm or distress. As with 'sus', police evidence will be sufficient to obtain a conviction. Hooliganism is in the eye of the beholder. Anyone for tennis?

Court orders, for people convicted at a football match or of a violent offence travelling to or from a match, would render them excluded from future matches for an unlimited period. Symbolically, too, putting riot, violent disorder and affray on to the statute book (they *were* always common law offences) warns 'rioting' fans of the *next* decade what they can expect. Kevin Whitton, a fan accused of participating in a savage pub brawl after a Man. United trip down South, could tell them it was pretty bad under the old system – he got 'life' for shaking his fist in the air until he was reprieved by the Appeal Court.

However, even if in the long run such wider control for fans is the outcome of Heysel '85, it doesn't mean that such measures will be successful anymore than FA prohibition of players' on-the-field behaviour can ever be said to 'work'. UEFA and FIFA bans on English clubs – and the threat of exclusion of the English national team if behaviour of club fans didn't improve – have meant enormous pressure on the civil and football authorities to both keep the lid on football's disorders and to make them as lacking in newsworthiness as possible if they do occur. Furthermore, the nostalgia for pre-Heysel Golden Days is so strong that it gets in the way of immediate memory. As the *Guardian* put it, Heysel soon got lost in a 'mist of forgetfulness':

> In the immediate aftermath of Brussels, Mrs Margaret Thatcher saw a great deal of soccer's leading statesmen. She is reliably reported to have been profoundly underwhelmed by their foresight and capabilities (though it is not recorded what they thought of her, or her unimpressive Sports Minister). Since those initial meetings, quite a lot has happened: but very little to make the Prime Minister happy.
>
> Take two developments. FIFA, the world body announces a wholesale ban on British clubs abroad. Then it calls the

whole thing off. Meanwhile, the Football Association appeals committee has been looking at the fines and penalties imposed on Luton and Millwall after last season's televized mayhem. Amazingly the appeals court finds both clubs blameless: fines are lifted and penalties greatly eased. So already a pattern is established at international and domestic level. Swingeing action whilst the horror is fresh: none too subtle reversals of all that once a thin film of forgetfulness has descended. Even Mr Neil Macfarlane, the aforementioned Sports Minister, is fuming.

The mists of forgetfulness soon descended on the public's memory of Mr Macfarlane (such as it was amongst football-goers) as he faded from the scene of high office but it was not only the various initiatives to combat disorder that went 'quiet' as the 1985-6 season got underway.

Nobody seems to have told Mrs Thatcher and Mr Justice Popplewell that the Casuals have increasingly in recent season been 'taking' rather more than ends. Luton v Millwall television footage should have confirmed for them that seats (and expensive seating at that) are 'in'. They make good missiles as television replays of Kenilworth Road told everybody, they are difficult to police effectively, they show you've got style, and most of all they make it easy to get away quickly (maybe slip out ten minutes before the end as so many 'respectable' fans do to get to their cars) to ambush the opposition crew who've been hemmed by the coppers all afternoon. And booze is out, too. Think sharp, look Sharp (with apologies to Man. United's shirt sponsors). *Stay* sharp to the bottom of the glass? Make mine *half* a lager!

Que sera, sera

Nowhere is Britain's current mood of fatalism – mixed with a startling complacency that assumes everything really will eventually be sorted out and normal (economic) service soon resumed – more evident than on the football pitches of League soccer. Talking to everyday professional players (not the 'stars') in the months after Heysel is like watching them perform on various 'parks' in diverse competitions over the last twenty years. Since 1966, the assumption that English (and by extension, depending on the occasion, 'British') is best, entangled with an obsessive deference to the 'boss' bordering on the masochistic, has pervaded footballers' language, dress, attitudes and playing styles ever since Geoff Hurst's hat-trick one (apparently) momentous afternoon. The cultural belief, of course, predated this by several centuries: but in footballing terms the notion used to have at least *some* credibility, even after the humiliating Hungarian defeats in the 1950s. After 1966 it was simply farce, and the images of Heysel relayed to ordinary footballers waiting back home for a new season finally got through. A new 'realism' has followed but one which effectively brings to the surface feelings which had been bubbling under since the 1960s. Kevin Keegan, as a player and as a sign of his times, epitomised this 'Englishness'. As Julie Burchill has pointed out:

> George Best was used as a bogeyman to scare the trusting children of football into a good living off the field.

The ironic corollary of this was that it became unacceptable even to attempt to *play* in the Best fashion. Flair was outlawed, resulting in a generation of drones, drilled into the ground by their coaches. The Goody-Goody Artisan syndrome was embodied by Kevin Keegan, a credit to his game (not to mention his species) but he was the *only* annotation in the profit margin of this new ethic that gripped the game. Of course, Mr Keegan's game had flashes of brilliance – and Best's work-rate and tackling were the two most underrated facets of his game – but when George hung up his boots, the fundamentals of the sport changed for ever. *Après* Best, football players, instead of striving to be artists, were not only content but expected – ordered! – to be workmanlike artisans.

Processes of transition from traditional to modern soccer styles however were never that straightforward in England. For sides outside the top bracket it was well into the 1970s by the time 4-3-3, 4-4-2 and the after-effects of the demise of the Busby era completely cramped their style. A player coming into the game in the 1972-3 season could still see flair, entertainment, skill as footballing values even if the top clubs (Liverpool, Arsenal, Leeds United) were espousing a very different route '66. Man. City, Man. United and Chelsea's bold attacking late 1960s teams were still powerful enough memories for lower division players and teams to look up to. There were still some 'free thinkers' around even by 1974 when, in the FA Cup final at Wembley, Liverpool and Keegan were making monkeys out of Malcolm Super(Mac)donald and Newcastle United – showing that with the right opposition they were no mugs; after all even Revie's robots contained individual players of the highest calibre, Johnny Giles and all.

Last of the Best

There were plenty of 'ordinary' players at lowly clubs in the early 1970s who had the skill to, say, spray Hoddle-like passes fifty yards across field: only they weren't considered as particularly outstanding by their professional colleagues or management. *Every* club side still had enough of such 'touch' players to make their play unremarkable.

Then the rot really set in. The style of the Arsenal double side of the early 1970s set the pattern for not just a few clubs but the wholesale restructuring of League football playing styles. The 'good' (by today's flair standards) started to be squeezed out and 'runners' – already on the increase – simply swept the board. Many more ordinary players (in terms of skill) started to get into the League teams at all levels that would have been beyond their wildest dreams a decade or so earlier. The balance between 'workers' and 'artists' in League soccer had shifted in a matter of a few years. The full back who could only wellie the ball into the stand, beloved of 1950s football watchers, may have been replaced by more skilful all-round footballers by the late 1970s but he was still performing the same routines, mainly because there were, in the rest of his side, so few players who could do anything with the ball in the event of them receiving a devastating through pass.

The reaction to the 1970s style revolution *did* occur in the 1980s. It was just that by then the skill and adventure came from either expensive overseas imports (Ardiles and Villa at Spurs, combined with Hoddle) or 'home-grown' black players who were given the monkey chant every time they touched the ball. The poorer clubs (and that meant most of the League by the early 1980s) couldn't afford to buy 'foreign' players. And since the managers' team talks still consisted of 'kick their black in the first twenty-five seconds' (a variation on the old 1950s theme of 'kick their winger in the first twenty-five seconds') it is still the case in the mid-1980s that the reintroduction of style and flair in League football has been limited to a precious few experiments amongst the higher flyers. 'Defensive' football, on the whole, has been justified by success rate. Lower clubs have invariably in the 1970s and 1980s achieved promotion, 'shock' cup wins and occasional trophies by aping the tried and trusted methods of their (bigger and) betters.

Exceptionally, Watford and Sheffield Wednesday and lately Wimbledon have soared towards the 'top' flight with a new, though backward looking, strategy. Though Wednesday, in particular, contradict their media image of thick Northerners with nothing between their ears kicking hell out of the ball because the 'boss' says so, what is significant about such percentage football (you're more likely to score in their third of the field than your own) is its relative success.

Wingers *as such* are no miracle cure for English club and national football's malaise; they need to know what they're doing and why they might be doing it. Third and Fourth division clubs have increasingly brought back wingers as publicity has spread about their resurrection through First division matches on 'live' television and the panic buttons have been hit in the wake of government measures which may severely cripple the game financially. Playing with two 'wingers' as a sop to the 'back to the Good Old Days' movement in British football, to entice the crowds back to The Shay, Vale Park, Spotland, and the County Ground, is a last desperate throw of the dice.

Ricky Villa playing against West Ham, 1982

Notts Forest striker Justin Fashanu at Arsenal, 1982

Clubs already destined to die, amalgamate or go part-time cling onto the old memories and dream of an Oxford-like rise to the twin towers and champagne lunches, whilst ground safety experts tell them that a high wind at the next home match would mean danger to their old stand and the game being abandoned. For players at this level (unless they have the added incentive of an international place with Wales, Scotland, Northern Ireland or Eire) it feels just as if soccer slavery had never gone away. The maximum wage may not have been formally re-introduced by edict, but they know that the same effect has been achieved by massively re-duced wage ceilings outside the 'elite'.

Up to mid-1984 eight clubs had wage bills of over £1 million. They included Brighton from the Second division but the rest – Arsenal, Man. United, Liverpool, Spurs, Everton, West Ham, Villa – were from the First division. The average wage bill in that period showed Second division clubs at £0.43 million, Third division £0.39 million and Fourth division £0.24 million whilst the First division weighed in with £1.02 million a year, some individual managers and players earning more than £80,000. For *most* professionals today Bryan Robson's job is light years away from their own. No wonder they prefer to read Fred Eyre and Eamon Dunphy than *George Best Rides Again*. As Brian Glanville put it in the preface to Dunphy's *Only A Game?*:

Eamon Dunphy's diary is the best and most authentic memoir by a professional footballer about his sport that I have yet read . . . Not that I feel we have been at last introduced to the 'true' football. There's as many truths about the game as there are about any other widely practised activity and Dunphy's own truth would clearly vary in accordance with the point in his career. In this case the point seems to be a

low one. Millwall, at the time, were not doing well, so the narrative tends to be tart. There is a latent feeling that not only Millwall but Dunphy himself, by then in his late twenties, have somehow missed the boat. An international footballer of skill and vision, he had still to play regularly in the First division, where he surely belonged. There is disillusionment with directors, managers, coaches, journalists, referees, fellow players, much dejection, little joy. Yet clearly it is hope that has soured, idealism that has been disappointed. Though no attempt is made to disguise the pro footballer's endemic paranoia, it is also plain that Dunphy knows how he feels the game should be played and approached, and is the more put out when it's exploited and distorted.

It is somewhat ironic that the decade since Dunphy's book has seen only Eyre's autobiographies (failed footballer, millionaire businessman) with the titles *Kicked into Touch* and *Another Breath Of* tell us about life with the 'Lions', 'Tigers' and the rest below stairs. Few publishers would take the risk of a 'true' autobiography from soccer's lower reaches. Who can blame the run-of-the-mill professional footballers of the 1980s for believing that 'someone up there wants to reduce the 92 clubs and make it not look like their fault'. They know – more acutely than did Dunphy in the 1970s – that they won't be 'going to Wembley' and that more than ever before 'whatever will be, will be'. 'All gone quiet over there?' ∎

7

Sing your hearts out for the lads

"And with me tonight, I have the former team manager, the captain of the '85 Cup winning side, and a gentleman from the FACE to comment on coming trends in football hodigan sportswear and accessories."

This book began with a cautionary tale about believing what is written in football books. The intervening pages are much more a 'book about football'. If it has made its mark it should have read like a 'live' game on TV rather than highlights later on 'Match of the Day'. Its peaks and troughs represent the ninety minutes (with extra time) of play – thrills and spills *plus* long periods of watching the fans because the numbing activity on the field drives you to distraction. The truth is that, as Fred and Judy Vermorel said about pop fans in their book *Starlust*, the current culture of fans in the 1980s is far more interesting than the star system. Football, more than any other entertainment, is living proof of this.

Steve Wagg's book *The Football World* has described footballers' lives in the 'age of publicity' but postmodern football culture – such as it is – has hardcore fans for whom Malcolm McLaren is more important than Marshall McLuhan. They may not be graduates of the arts schools (not many anyway) but post-punk influences on football and style continue to make their presence felt. Casual styles are now widely disseminated across the country's young football fans (and many young professionals) in a never-ending procession of phases – a Nike or Burberry period here, a wedge or Terry McDermott 'perm' there – since the ebb of the initial shock waves of punk. The term 'Casual' itself is more usual currency in journalistic circles; newshounds desperate for a new angle on football violence have seized on it only to find that its use is already outdated and its style leaders have become *less* fashion-conscious just as the men (nearly always) from the 'meeja' think they really know what's going on 'out there'. No sooner does someone tell them that Man. United's fighting crew is called 'The Red Army' than they have to cope with factions representing themselves (depending on how gullible they think the listener is) as 'Cockney Reds', 'SS' or 'Inter-City Train Jibbers'. Once they've got the hang of the Maine Line Crew, along come new pretenders coming on dressed as the 'Young Governors' of Maine Road. Once Millwall's 'The Treatment' or 'F-Troop' sounds plausible, the harassed hack is despatched by his editor to interview the 'Bushwackers'. The 'Gooners' sounds near enough to Arsenal's nickname to avoid confusion but how does he know the 'Kenton Bar Boys' are telling him Geordie hometruths when they claim to have gone straight to the top of the 'nutters' league. In this pantomime of media coverage one thing is certain: the 'Well, Brian' joke is well and truly turned on those who laughed loudest at it in the first place, even if it took the fans rather than the players to play it in the 1980s.

'Style' was always going to be a difficult weapon to wield in football. A 'new authenticity' was quietly lurking up around the next bend and 'content' constantly threatened to rear its ugly head. In 1985 – the official year of football's death – 'serious lyrics' started to become fashionable in pop music. Partly a reaction to the 'pretty boy' new pop era which followed punk in Britain, it was also an aspect of the ever increasing 'Americanization' of British pop culture. Professional football stuck its head in the sand – with the exception of a few marching bands as pre-match entertainment – and the Superbowl looted the ratings at the expense of 'The Big Match' 'live'.

It is still, though, the punk explosion of 1976-7 which marks a watershed in pop. Johnny Rotten and Sid Vicious stand on the graves of John Lennon and Paul McCartney: the Sex Pistols rather than the Beatles are the benchmark for the resurrection of pop's spirit of rebellion – '76 not '67.

Whether the new authenticity can resist the temptations of fame and fortune which finally

" We may have post-modernist fans, but our team are unremittingly
HEAVY METAL!"

demolished 1960s rock myths during the 1970s is now on the agenda. The trouble with the history of pop culture (music and football in particular) is that when it repeats itself in a new decade – in a new setting – there are already plenty of ghosts waiting in the wings to do an encore. The same tired, clapped-out clichés (musical and political) surfaced as part of 'Live Aid' in 1985. Only Elvis Costello seemed to understand the ironies of a multitude gathered in a field. He introduced the Beatles' 'All You Need Is Love' to an audience of billions as 'an old English folk song' and proceeded to hammer out a savage epitaph to hippie idealism on a lone amplified guitar – shades of Billy Bragg, who still imagines that he's The Clash rather than James Taylor when he gets up on stage. Wembley/Philadelphia 'nation' looked pretty much like Woodstock to a wandering minstrel who'd cut his musical teeth on Stiff tours. For *anyone* who had a sense of cultural history, though, it was easy to see the times had changed. As David Toop pointed out in *The Face*, black music was significant by its almost total absence and the overwhelming effect was to confirm white superiority even in the very moment of giving millions of pounds to starving Africans. Ethnic 'folk' musics, too, didn't fare so well which makes Costello's version of the old hippie anthem doubly telling.

In many ways, though, it is football culture itself which has the last remaining authentic 'folk' songs in Thatcher's Britain. Northern 'old English folk songs' sound more like odes to our leader than the proto-socialism beloved of folk revivalists. Man. City fans chanted taunts at Yorkshire and Welsh teams during (and after) the miners' strike which included:

Arthur Scargill
Is a wanker, is a wanker

and:

Get back to work you lazy twats

not to mention:

You only wish you were mining.

Just as they seemed more like cabinet replacements for sacked or resigning ministers, they greeted fans from Nottingham with:

You scab bastards,
You scab bastards.

Regionalism, reflecting and deepening the new geography of labour (and unemployment) that characterizes Britain in the 1980s, is far more important in generating 'songs' for football fans than any simple 'right' or 'left' wing political commitment. Songs on the terraces have a history, too, in that there is a definite post-punk character to the style of football songs in the 1980s marking them out from the earlier 'Beatles' phase in the 1960s ('Ee-Ay-Adio' and 'You'll Never Walk Alone'). But it is their roots in the dire straits of 'no futurism' that really matters now. 'He's Only a Poor Little Scouser' has replaced the Merseybeat back catalogue. And young working-class scallies, Mancs or Cockneys smoking joints in the toilets, courtesy of stolen tickets from British Rail, is as apt a comment on the 1960s myths (peace, love and the 'white heat' of Harold Wilson's industrial strategy) as Elvis Costello's wry look back at the 'fab four'.

If football's style politics are such a smart sign of the times, such a good barometer of Britain's domestic and international malaise, what price the rebirth of a democratic sport from the ruins of Heysel and Bradford City stadiums? Football, as the story in this book has demonstrated, is not always about team photos and little homilies on sportsmanship from Jimmy Hill and Bob Wilson. The hilarious picture of the people's longest running chat and game show (The Price *isn't* Right but come on down anyway), without 'professional fouls', personal vendettas, feigned injury and 'industrial' language, presented for public consumption by our guardians of soccer morality, not only lulls the nation into a false sense of security ('Heysel' – shock, horror). It also predictably, invites the 'fun-for-all-the-family' solutions for forgetful nostalgia buffs. What is creative, spontaneous and (for a minute or two) uncontrolled in football's pleasures punctures the spectacle occasionally but it is always already under control. Hints of a crisis in the masculine image of the sport are blotted out with quick flashes of real, tough men winning wars and battles, even if it means young black and white designer gangs throwing seats at the boys in blue. The obituary notices have gone up but the people's 'art' refuses to lie down and die.

Police chiefs do their best to tell us that emergency government measures are working and FA officials hope that soon English clubs will be back 'terrorizing' Europeans on their own soil: putting them in their place again just like the prime minister.

What is to be done about football? Precious few organized responses have made much impact. The Anti-Nazi League campaigns in the wake of punky reggae parties in the 1970s had some successes but the National Front and its bedfellows have lived on well into the 1980s at and around football stadia, as leaflets blowing in the wind at Heysel's battleground once again emphasized. At least one *Foul* successor, *Off The Ball*, rose from the ashes of the death of modern football in 1985 and the Football Supporters Association has tried to mobilize popular support amongst 'ordinary' spectators. Those who think this hour is a little late for such action should put their feet up and watch the telly as Bryan Robson limps off (again), only to be substituted by a blip on a video screen, and think of football (and the nation) as they knew it.

Laughter – as this book has indicated – is one of the few collective resistances to the banality and sheer incompetence of much of today's League soccer style. When football fans (and players) wake up to realize that football in England – and English football – without the Empire is a serious case of an undressed Emperor (perhaps he never did have any clothes, even in the early post-war days), the laughter has a hollow ring about it. In this context 'genuine' football fanzines like *When Saturday Comes* are as much a caricature of traditional football writing as the 'match lads', 'Gucci boys', 'neo-Herberts' (or whatever epithet you care to think of) are of watching football. Where are you now *Roy of the Rovers*?

But laughter and the in-jokes of expensive menswear are never going to be enough to re-

The glory days

build an industry close to the brink. The cultural politics of the carefully aimed (two-fingered) gesture is all very well but it soon reduces itself to impotent violence (once again). It is only one aspect of postmodern football in any case. Precious little is written or said from the standpoint, say, of teenage girl fans – apart from Julie Welch's homage to Danny Blanchflower and Spurs' olden, golden days – in any era. For League soccer to be worth saving it has to relinquish its roots in long traditions of all-male culture. Modern football simply inherited such traditions as it did the mythologies of how and why the game should be played and organized. The only style that counts in the long term for football in the 'mother country' is that of the game itself. The hi-speed, neurotic race which generally characterizes English play in the mid-1980s – encouraged by fans weaned on goal highlights every few seconds – is symptomatic of its organization: desperate, confused, aimless, guided by misplaced beliefs in outmoded heroes and conventions, and deeply suspicious of outside advice. Soccer style may not always reflect national or regional culture in any simple way. But this book certainly would have been different if it had been about Scotland or Ireland rather than about England (and the way that Welsh, Irish and Scottish influences resonate over the hundred years of League soccer), or if it had not been written from within the North West at a time when other hard-hit regions (such as the North East or Midlands) are going through the footballing doldrums.

National soccer styles do matter. The best example of this is still Brazil. Though England won the World Cup in 1966 the most significant consequence for World soccer was Brazil's exit from the competition as a result both of a lowering of its previously high standards of ball play and the violent, destructive, calculating cynicism of some of their opponents. The match of the tournament was surely Hungary's magnificent eclipse of the world champions (East European dash against South American langour) one rainy night in Liverpool. The massed crowd at Goodison Park who stood to applaud *both* teams as they disappeared to the changing rooms didn't only reflect the region's reputation for appreciating 'away' teams' excellence. However incorporated that game was into the jingoistic melodrama that saw England replay the Second World War at Wembley (blond German youth against true Brit grit) those fans knew the difference between honest commitment and unbridled style. Before we swallow the Latin footballing myths – all samba rhythm and 'natural' talent – we should remember what followed 1966. Brazil, poleaxed more by the viciousness of the other teams in their group than by the brilliance of the Hungarians, made up for their early exit by winning the 1970 World Cup in Mexico, handsomely and with a panache and joy that is not dimmed by endless TV repeats of their defeat of Italy in the Final itself. However, they too adopted overtly violent tactics in West Germany in the 1974 tournament fearing – a neat reversal of prejudices, this – a repeat of the brutal 'European' style they had experienced in 1966. For the sake of soccer it was fortunate that they were again eliminated, heralding a return to the graceful style of play which is so clearly their logo, though it was Argentina – as representatives of a continent renowned in football folklore for its fighting as much as its finesse – who took the eye (and the trophy) in 1978 in overcoming the European flair of Holland's 'total' football, the emerging France of Platini, and the rest, and again in 1986 with Maradona's outstanding performance, eclipsing Scifo, Laudrup and all.

What is important for English football, at nat-ional and international level, is the ample demonstration twenty years on from 1966 that the 'chance' corollary of the United Kingdom's relegation to the third division of industrial powers is decline in England's football status. The resistance to such demotion leads to today's absurdist text that the 'experts' say passes for professional football: national and club sides floundering against opposition they shouldn't even be playing! Jimmy Greaves' instant response to the USSR row with England over travel arrangements to Tbilisi for a friendly international in 1986 was (effectively) that the 'comrades' should 'shove it'. There were plenty of other willing sparring partners and if the 'Ruskies' couldn't play by the rules, administrative action should be taken against them. Back in the UK!

The most lasting effect of this insular policy is the organization of football at home. If ever there was a case of the blind leading the bland this is it. When in 1982 Sir Norman Chester, first recruited to report on the state of soccer back in 1968, accepted a second invitation to investigate ways of reforming the structure of League football, he remarked:

> Quite a lot has changed in the last 14 years. From what I have read and seen the atmosphere of the game is different. Then the public were still cock-a-hoop after England's World Cup victory in 1966. Today people are worried about the finance of the game ... Finance and the image of the game are probably the most important problems.

Chester's second report has, in effect, gone the same way as the first – into the (permanently) pending tray – whilst events have overtaken the proposals. A report published by the Football Trust (deputy chairman, Sir Norman) in 1986

1966 and all that

calculated that at the present rate of decline no one would be watching Football League matches by the year 2015. Chester's own view that 'everybody who professes an interest in football should spend at least one Sunday morning on Hackney Marshes and one Saturday afternoon watching Hartlepool or Brechin', expressed in 1982, had altered somewhat as the 1980s progressed. In what might be regarded as an epitaph for professional soccer more than a hundred years after the first players took money home from a game legitimately, Chester commented that many lower division clubs could not go on existing with an income below the inflation rate. He said, further that:

> Many of these clubs are relying heavily on subsidies from sponsorship and television to exist and it would mean they would have to go part-time if they were not in the League. I cannot see why attendances should ever go back to the higher level of the 60s, or the 70s. It seems to me there is a need to concentrate resources on fewer clubs.

Football 1990 is glimpsed here without regret. There is no going back to kicking a tennis ball against a wall on a cobbled street in a mining village to bring back the Golden Age of English football; there is no 'return' to original authenticity. Unless style can be turned into revolt, football for the rest of the century will increasingly borrow its weapons from other sports (billiard balls, darts, golf balls with nails, sharpened half-pennies, starting pistols) for its ever more vicious and hopeless manoeuvres and derive sustenance from the economic and military strategy of late Thatcherism. The diverse pleasures of football playing and watching in the past are fast being phased out altogether leaving a bewildered nation wondering merely whether

it's safe to go back to the local ground again, one last time, before the removal men and the business spivs fight over the hallowed turf. Much has happened between Munich '58 and Mexico '86 but is it really too late to save soccer from its monetarist grave? *Now* you're going to believe us? ■

Soccer's sale of the century

My back pages

(or what to read when your local game is next played behind closed doors)

Books:
There *are* some worthwhile football books but they are very rarely seen on the bookshelves. These are the lovingly prepared club histories which only fans read and which make no money for anybody. The best of the rest are:

Patrick Barclay, *From Schoolboy to Superstar*, Harmondsworth: Puffin 1983.

Hunter Davies, *The Glory Game*, Edinburgh: Mainstream 1985.

Eamon Dunphy (with Peter Ball), *Only A Game? The Diary of A Professional Footballer*, Harmondsworth: Peacock 1977.

Fred Eyre, *Another Breath Of . . .*, Glossop: Senior 1982.
Kicked Into Touch, Glossop: Senior 1981.

Jimmy Guthrie (with Dave Caldwell), *Soccer Rebel: The Evolution of the Professional Footballer*, London: Davis Foster 1976.

Arthur Hopcraft, *The Football Man: People and Passions in Soccer*, Harmondsworth: Penguin 1971.

John Hutchinson, *The Football Industry: The Early Years of the Professional Game*, Glasgow: Richard Drew 1982.

Anton Rippon, *Soccer: The Road to Crisis*, Derby: Moorland 1983.

David Robins, *We Hate Humans*, Harmondsworth: Penguin 1984.

Steve Wagg, *The Football World*, Brighton: Harvester 1984.

Andrew Ward and Ian Alister, *Barnsley: A Study in Football 1953-1959*, Staffordshire: Crowberry 1981.

Gordon Williams and Terry Venables, *They Used To Play On Grass*, London: Mayflower 1973.

Magazines

Foul magazine is now long dead but there is a collection of 'golden oldies' in *The Foul Book of Football No 1: The Best of Foul, 1972-5*, Cambridge: Foul Publications 1976.

Off The Ball available from 487, Bristol Road, Selly Oak, Birmingham B29 6AU

When Saturday Comes available from 157 Robinson Road, London SW17 9NS

Programmes

Most football match programmes reflect football culture about as much as sheepskin coats sum up football fashions but there is a good account of their importance in Phil Shaw, *Collecting Football Programmes*, London: Granada 1980.